# Le français, c'est facile!

## Strategies and Resources for Special Needs

# Acknowledgements

Many thanks to Les Moore without whom the resources pack would never have been produced, since he provided all of the initial pictures from the very earliest stages of the project. He has also spent many hours listening to, and commenting on, ideas as they have occurred.

We would also like to acknowledge the invaluable support and expertise of the following:

Teachers of French in Hampshire Special Schools;

Ron Jennings, Teacher Adviser MFL;

Marilyn Summons for her assistance in processing the text.

# Le français, c'est facile!

## Strategies and Resources for Special Needs

**Sue Brown**
Stoke Damerel Community College, Plymouth
**Sue Dean**
Hampshire County Council

JOHN MURRAY

© Sue Brown, Hampshire County Council 1995
First published 1995 by John Murray (Publishers) Ltd
50 Albemarle Street, London W1X 4BD

A CIP record for this book is available from the British Library.


Cover design by John Townson/Creation

Layouts by Mick McCarthy

Illustrations by David Anstey

Typeset by Wearset, Boldon, Tyne & Wear

Printed in Great Britain by St Edmundsbury Press,
Bury St Edmunds

ISBN 0 7195 7100 6

● ● ● ● ● ● ● ● ● ● ● ● ● ● ● ● ● ● ● ● ● ● ● ● ● ● ● ● ● ● ● ● ● ● ● ● ● ● ● ●

# Contents

# General introduction

With the National Curriculum statement that, 'In principle all pupils with special educational needs should have the opportunity to experience a modern foreign language', a languages for all policy became a reality, and not before time. However, this positive move created the need for foreign languages to be made accessible for the whole ability range, and it was from this need that the Le français, c'est facile! resource was developed.

## Who is it for?

### The pupils involved

More than 30% of pupils experience learning difficulties at school; as they excitedly begin French in year 7, they require a resource to meet their particular needs. This resource aims to interest, motivate and successfully teach them.

The some 2% of pupils with Special Needs statements will be mainly in Special Schools, although increasingly they are integrated into mainstream schools; some will already be in mainstream, with close links with its Special Needs Department. The majority of the target pupils will, however, be in mainstream without the extra support that a statement brings.

Amongst all of these pupils there will be many with very specific, individual needs in French, which a variety of teaching and support staff will need to meet.

### The teaching staff involved

In Special Schools the policy of entitlement in languages has given rise to a situation in which many teachers whose expertise is in Special Needs teaching rather than language teaching are faced with providing, in a very limited time, the best they can by way of an introduction to French and the French way of life. This is often being done with great enthusiasm and energy, but also on a shoe-string budget, and without enough time for planning or for the preparation of resources. This resource aims to provide an affordable, accessible pack of materials which will supply these teachers with most of what they need to plan and to resource their French teaching for Key Stage 3.

In mainstream schools non-linguist staff in Special Needs Departments are often providing support for pupils in years 7, 8 and 9, explaining, simplifying and generally differentiating materials on the spot or, at best, for the next lesson. The pack hopes to provide Special Needs Departments with a flexible, clear resource which staff can tailor to individual needs.

Modern Languages Departments in most mainstream schools may have plenty of resources that staff can dip into to create differentiated material for pupils with various learning difficulties. What they, too often, do not have is the time to do this or to make the activities attractive. Moreover, with the materials available, they may not be able to differentiate sufficiently to cater appropriately for the least able. For these teachers this resource provides a ready source of worksheets and activities which take only minutes to make up, and which can be virtually individually tailored.

## The value of using Le français, c'est facile!

### Linguistic values

- Pupils will experience success through learning and using French, the success in itself being as important as the obvious functional value of being able to operate in a foreign language.
- More generally, they may also experience:
  - training for listening
  - re-learning to read
  - practice in copy-writing and writing from memory.
  i.e. general linguistic development which may have been missed in early childhood.
- All of these experiences happen in a friendly, stress-free, supportive environment, which is very conducive to the development of language skills.

### Educational values

- The resource aids general learning through developing cross-curricular links and skills.
- It aids and improves memory.
- It enables pupils to communicate more effectively.
- It allows the recycling of concepts not previously understood, without loss of self-esteem.
- It provides a challenge.
- It helps to fulfil the right of every pupil to a broad and balanced curriculum.

### Personal and social values

- It encourages pupils to work in co-operation with others, as well as individually.
- It develops self-confidence through success. Steps are small and manageable and can be achieved regularly and often.
- It widens experiences and, therefore, horizons.
- It gives opportunities for learned social behaviour (through simulation, role plays, etc.).

- It encourages tolerance and understanding of other people and other cultures.
- It increases self-esteem through the opportunities for achievement and success.

# The components of *Le français, c'est facile!*

The following list is a brief summary of the components of this resource. For details of how the resource should be used, see the **Practical introductions** on pages 13–18.

- **A detailed Scheme of Work** for the nine modules, i.e. a structured framework for planning, including communicative and linguistic objectives, and setting out suggested resources, activities and final assignments. The Scheme of Work also outlines opportunities for assessment and explains how the resource is designed to meet the requirements of the National Curriculum.
- **Pictures** which exactly match the vocabulary included, and which can be easily reduced or enlarged to use with a whole variety of suggested activities (see pages 163–188).
- **Worksheet templates** for a variety of practice, reinforcement and assessment activities (see pages 20–45).
- **Suggestions for games** and the templates for making these, using the pictures supplied (see pages 47–91).
- Other **photocopy masters** for classroom use.
- **Teaching notes** at the end of each of the modules giving details of any content or methodology not previously explained in the introduction to the resources and activities.
- **Explanatory notes** on all of these materials written with non-linguist teachers in mind.

# Special features of *Le français, c'est facile!*

## Flexibility

- Within the suggested linguistic objectives (vocabulary and phrases) for each module, teachers can choose the most relevant and appropriate elements as well as tailor the amount of content to the group or individual.
- The pictures have a large number of suggested uses but teachers may use them as they wish, with a wide range of sizes available. They may also be copied onto OHT or can be used to make concept keyboard overlays.
- Within the suggested activities teachers may again pick and choose depending on the interest, needs, behaviour and mood of the group, or the time available, and on the timing of the lesson in the day or the week.

- Worksheets cover a variety of skills and levels and all but Set 1 lend themselves to a wide variety of uses.
- The games come with suggestions for playing them at various levels and teachers or pupils will inevitably think up new variations of old games.
- Topics and linguistic objectives are regularly revisited, giving pupils either the opportunity to learn again what was not fully understood the first time or to re-use known material in a new situation or context. (See content mapping matrix on page 12.)

## Ease of use

- The materials have been produced in such a way that teachers, support staff or classroom assistants should be able quickly and easily to make up worksheets, activities or games, as and when individuals or small groups need them, as well as the general preparation of whole class materials for the basic Scheme of Work.
- Blank templates serve as an outline for production of materials.
- Pictures are produced on an easy sliding scale of reproduction for either enlargement or reduction.
- The instructions for use, in the general introduction to the resources and in teaching notes for each module, are clear and straightforward.
- The Scheme of Work framework provides invaluable guidelines for planning in both the short and the long term.
- Many teachers will appreciate the suggestions for assessment since they cover a range of Attainment Targets and levels for each topic.

## The *Le français, c'est facile!* song cassette and booklet

(ISBN 0 7195 7110 3)

Once pupils have become familiar with the basic vocabulary of a particular topic, this cassette and booklet pack offers opportunities to add an extra dimension to their listening and oral work. The 60-minute cassette includes (on Side 1) the fourteen 'Framework songs' listed below.

These are written around a limited vocabulary based on the linguistic objectives given for the topics in this resource file. For each song, guidelines are given to enable teachers to vary the vocabulary and the theme of the song, while retaining the familiar basic structure and tune. The tunes without words are supplied on Side 2 of the cassette to allow variations of the vocabulary to be used.

All the songs and activities have been either written or adapted by Elissa Collins, to provide the structure, rhythm, musical range and pace to suit the needs of pupils with learning difficulties.

The resources box on each topic sheet indicates when use of the cassette is recommended.

## IT opportunities

*Le français, c'est facile!* can also be used in conjunction with various IT packages, such as *Le français sous la main* (a concept-keyboard based package published jointly by John Murray and North West Semerc —details available from John Murray) or *Le monde à*

**Relationship between the framework songs and their variants and the modules in *Le français, c'est facile!***

| Module number in *Le français c'est facile!* | 1 | 2 | 3 | 4 | 5 | 6 | 7 | 8 | 9 |
|---|---|---|---|---|---|---|---|---|---|
| L'alphabet | ✓ | | | | | | | | |
| Les jours | | | ✓ | | | | | | |
| Bonjour et au revoir | ✓ | | | | | | ✓ | ✓ | |
| Les numéros | ✓ | | | | ✓ | | | | |
| Directions | | | ✓ | ✓ | | | ✓ | | |
| Gentil Coquelicot | | ✓ | | ✓ | | | | | |
| Variants | | ✓ | | ✓ | | ✓ | | | ✓ |
| Super rap | | | ✓ | | | | | | |
| Variants | | ✓ | ✓ | | ✓ | ✓ | | ✓ | ✓ |
| La maison de Marjolaine | | | | ✓ | | | ✓ | | |
| Variants | ✓ | ✓ | ✓ | | ✓ | ✓ | ✓ | | ✓ |
| Au café | | | | | ✓ | ✓ | | | |
| Variants | | | | | ✓ | ✓ | ✓ | ✓ | ✓ |
| À la boulangerie | | | | | ✓ | | | | |
| Variants | | | | | ✓ | ✓ | ✓ | ✓ | |
| Bon voyage | | | | | ✓ | | | | |
| Variants | | | | | ✓ | | | | |
| Enchanté | | ✓ | | | | | ✓ | | |
| Variants | ✓ | | | | | | ✓ | | |
| Savez-vous planter | | | | | | | | ✓ | |
| Variants | | | | | | | | ✓ | |
| Gagnez de l'argent | | | | | | | | | ✓ |
| Variants | | | | | | ✓ | | | ✓ |

*moi*. The resources box on some topic sheets indicates when suitable opportunities arise to make use of such packages.

# Vocabulary/linguistic objectives

- For each topic there is a list of some 20–25 words deemed essential for effectively teaching the topic. These are suggested examples and teachers may wish to add or substitute their own items, but the lists given form the basis of the topic activities.
- Occasionally the list is longer since the topic invites the teacher to tailor the list to the needs of the class/individual.
- Sometimes there are also extra receptive/ productive phrases which can, again, be used at the discretion of the teacher.
- The vocabulary has been selected to aid pupils as much as possible so, when two words exist in English and French in similar forms, the English word is chosen. (This is sometimes a compromise but it is realistic.)
- Words are listed in alphabetical order unless there is an obvious sequence of use, e.g. phrases for dialogues.
- Words are listed with definite articles, although, with some pupils, use of articles at all may be inappropriate. What is deemed communicative is always left to the discretion of the teacher and will depend on individual pupils' difficulties, etc.

# Flashcard presentation of vocabulary

- The use of flashcards, where appropriate, facilitates understanding without the need to translate.
- Stages of flashcard presentation:
  - Show the image and say the word.
  Class then individuals repeat. This stage needs a lot of repetition.
  - Show the image and ask: *C'est A?*
  This elicits simple response: *Oui/Non*.
  - Show the image and ask: *C'est A ou B?*
  This elicits response: *(Oui.) C'est A. (Non.) C'est B*, etc.
  - Finally ask: *Qu'est-ce que c'est?*
  For response: *C'est A/B*, etc.

# Use of cue cards for vocabulary

- Teachers need to make simple clear cue cards for flashcards used.
- These printed or handwritten labels (lower-case!) can then be linked with pictures once they are known orally, to introduce reading.
- Flashcards can be displayed around the room/on the board.
- Stages of use for cue cards:
  - Put cue card with appropriate picture. Say word. Class/individual repetition.
  - Then show just cue card. Say word. Class/individual repetition.
  - Show cue card. Class/individuals supply word and/or place it with picture.
  - The class is then ready for the basic worksheets.

# Practical introduction to the Scheme of Work

The framework for *Le français, c'est facile!* is based on the structure of HANSOW; this is a KS3 Scheme of Work for modern foreign languages produced over a period of 18 months by the Hampshire advisory service working in co-operation with over 70 MFL teachers in a series of Inset sessions. The original Scheme of Work was published in 1992, having met its objectives of allowing teachers to plan collectively for the National Curriculum, and of contributing to curriculum development.

It soon became clear that this curriculum plan had benefits beyond its intended mainstream audience. Teachers in Special Schools had already begun to plan in their own schools for meeting their pupils' entitlement to a modern foreign languages experience, and to take part in Inset on modern languages methodology. The need for a coherent context for this work led the teacher advisers for MFL to set up a conference with Special School MFL teachers to investigate the adaptation of HANSOW to match the learning needs of pupils, and the time restraints on the curriculum in Special Schools.

The conference was attended by representatives from over 75% of Hampshire's Special Schools with KS3 pupils with moderate learning difficulties (MLD) or emotional and behavioural difficulties (EBD). The resulting development of the HANSOW SPECIAL Scheme of Work has been characterized by co-operation, and a meeting of minds and experiences. The Scheme of Work has been piloted in Special Schools, reviewed and amended. It is, of course, also designed for use in mainstream schools alongside main course material. Indeed, colleagues in many mainstream schools have expressed interest in using the Special Schools' framework; it would be of particular relevance in planning for differentiation within the mainstream framework.

## Structure

The structure of the Scheme of Work is modular, that is to say, it is divided into units of work each relating to a particular area of interest for pupils. There are nine modules; each one has several linked topics. There has been an attempt to revise and re-cycle language through the Scheme of Work, but this should not prevent teachers from changing the order of topics or modules, or from substituting their own ideas in order to suit the circumstances in their particular school. It was assumed at the outset that each module would last approximately one term, but indications from teachers are that this will vary from school to school, that flexibility is essential, and even that some of the topics will be more appropriate in KS4.

## Assignments

It was clear from the start that teachers want to concentrate on what their pupils can do with the language they have learned; this is why outcomes from pupils are expressed in terms of communicative **objectives**. In keeping with this principle, possible assignments have been suggested for each module. These are intended to provide a purpose for the work in a module, and ideally have in mind the idea of an 'audience'.

## National Curriculum Orders

The Scheme of Work has been checked for compatibility with the new orders for MFL and some amendments have been made to ensure that it is completely up to date.

## Areas of experience

In KS3, pupils must explore areas of experience A, B and C – **Everyday activities**, **Personal and social life**, and **The world around us**. In KS4, pupils following a full course revisit areas A, B and C and also explore areas D and E – **The world of work** and **The international world**. On each module sheet there is an indication of the areas of experience to which the module is most clearly relevant.

## Programme of Study (part 1)

The examples given have been amended to match the opportunities for pupils required in **part 1, Learning and Using the Target Language**. It must be stressed that these are examples only.

## Attainment targets and level descriptions

There are opportunities for work in all four ATs, though with less emphasis on AT4 (writing) than on the other three targets. The examples given as **Opportunities for Assessment** are compatible with the level descriptions.

## Cross-curricular opportunities

The examples provided are to highlight where opportunities exist for teachers to reinforce aspects of their work with pupils across the boundaries of subjects. These are not statutory.

# Mapping of linguistic objectives

This cross-referencing of content indicates where revision naturally occurs and also where known material is used in new contexts.

| Topic | | | | | | | |
|---|---|---|---|---|---|---|---|
| Greetings | 1(i) | 7(i) | | | | | |
| Naming | 1(ii) | 2(i) | 7(i) | | | | |
| Classroom objectives | 1(iii) | Throughout Module 3 | | | | | |
| Classroom target language | 1(iv) | Constant reinforcement | | | | | |
| Alphabet | 1(v) | Constant reinforcement | | | | | |
| Numbers | 1(v) | 4(iii) | 5(iv) | 9(i) | | | |
| Family members | 2(i) | 6(i) | 7(i) | | | | |
| Parts of the body | 2(ii) | 8(iii) | | | | | |
| Colours | 2(ii) | 2(iii) | 4(v) | 5(iii) | 9(iii) | | |
| Pets | 2(iii) | 7(i) | | | | | |
| Likes and dislikes | 2(iv) | 3(ii) | 3(iii) | 5(iii) | 6(ii) | 7(iii) | 8(iii) |
| Days of the week | 3(iii) | 6(i) | 6(iii) | 7(iii) | 8(i) | | |
| Position | 3(iv) | 4(iv) | 5(ii) | 7(ii) | | | |
| House (exterior) | 4(i) | 7(ii) | | | | | |
| Rooms | 4(iii) | 6(ii) | 7(ii) | | | | |
| Furniture | 4(v) | 6(i) | 6(ii) | | | | |
| Transport | 5(i) | 7(iv) | | | | | |
| Shops | 5(ii) | 7(iii) | 9(ii) | | | | |
| Food | 5(iii) | 6(ii) | | | | | |
| Money | 5(iv) | 9(i) | | | | | |
| Shopping | 5(v) | 9(ii) | | | | | |
| Activities | 6(i) | 8(i) | | | | | |
| Places in town | 7(iii) | 8(i) | 9(i) | | | | |
| Hobbies | 8(i) | 9(ii) | | | | | |

# Practical introduction to the resources and activities

The explanations given below on how to use the various components are common to all modules or topics, and will not be repeated in the teaching notes for each topic. The teaching notes that are given for each individual topic are brief guidelines and suggestions specific to the use of resources and activities for that particular topic. All of the resources are uniquely flexible and the uses specified are merely suggestions.

The resources comprise the following:

- Sheets of pictures with the French words on the reverse, linked to lists of vocabulary in the modules/topics. These are provided at the correct size for worksheet use and can be enlarged for games, flashcards, etc.
- Blank templates for worksheets (three sets allowing for differentiation and progression). **Note:** samples of the worksheets are made up ready for use as examples.
- Blank masters for activities and games (excluding bingo). **Note:** samples of selected games/activities are made up as examples (see pages 56–61). Individual topic templates for bingo:
  1. School bag (for classroom objects)
  2. Garden (for animals)
  3–5. Timetables (for school subjects)
  6. House (for furniture)
  7. Basket (for food)
  8. Snack menu (for food and drinks)
  9. Town plan (for places in the town)
  10. Tablecloth (for laying the table)
  11. Case (for clothes)
  12. Body (for parts of the body)
  13. Palette (for colours).
- Photocopy masters for shops, days of the week, e.g. for wall display.
- The **Resources** box on the topic sheets is divided into two. The items in the lower section are not supplied.

As has been stated, the aim of this teaching pack is that it should be as flexible as possible. So, although activities are suggested for each topic, the pictures and blank templates that are provided allow teachers quickly and easily to produce tailor-made activities to suit individual needs.

## How to use the pictures

Each topic has one, sometimes two, sheets of pictures, one for each of the vocabulary items listed in the Linguistic objectives box on the topic sheet. Blank squares mark the end of each subject area. These master sheets show a maximum of 32 pictures. The pictures are intended to be photocopied at a variety of sizes (always on the principle of A4 to A3 or vice versa, as some photocopying equipment offers only this factor of enlargement or reduction). By this process, the pictures can be adapted for a variety of different uses. The table on page 14 shows how this works.

## How to use the worksheets

### ◆ SET 1

**Format**
- Thick outlines indicate that the picture is to be affixed; edges also prevent shadow when photocopying cut-outs.
- Thin outlines mean that a picture is to be drawn in by the pupil.
- Double lines for writing indicate that writing is to be copied.
- Single lines for writing mean that the teacher or the pupil (depending on the exercise) is to supply the written word.

**Note:** teachers may find it useful to code these sheets by using different coloured paper for sheets within sets; or they may prefer to code modules/topics by colour, keeping the worksheets within sections the same.

### Use

These four sheets are central to the early stages of learning for each topic. Because they are regularly used, pupils become familiar with the format, understand what is required, and feel secure and confident. The sheets should be used at appropriate times in the early stages of a topic, but not all at once.

**Variety is important** Pupils soon have the confidence to choose which sheets to do, and even go back to ones they feel the need to revise.

### Activities and National Curriculum mapping
**Sheet 1**
- *Copie les mots et les images*
  Copy the words and the pictures [AT4:1]
The idea of some kind of recognizable image being produced is to enable understanding to be checked without recourse to the written word or translation. It also encourages the correct copying of the word.
**Sheet 2**
- *Lis les mots et dessine les images*
  Read the words and draw the pictures [AT3:1]
This shows understanding of the written word.

## Resources and activities

| Enlargement/ reduction at each stage | | Approximate size of individual picture/mm | Number of pictures/ sheet A4 | A3 | Uses of pictures |
|---|---|---|---|---|---|
| A3 ↑ A4 | x141% | 251 x 178 | 1 | 2 | Flashcards |
| | x141% | 178 x 126 | 2 | 4 | Small flashcards, display |
| | x141% | 126 x 90 | 4 | 8 | Large games cards, display |
| | x141% | 90 x 64 | 8 | 16 | Snap cards, etc. |
| | x141% | 64 x 45 | 16 | 32 | |
| Photocopy master | | 45 x 32 | 32 | 64 | Basic worksheets |
| A4 ↓ A5 | x71% | 32 x 23 | 64 | 128 | Wordsearch, survey, etc. |
| | x71% | 23 x 16 | | 128 | – |

**Note:**
1. All enlargements are 141% i.e. A4 → A3.
2. All reductions are 71% i.e. A4 → A5.
3. A 90° rotation of the pictures occurs on each enlargement, therefore only half the photocopied sheet is reproduced.
   The other half must be photocopied separately.
4. A 90° rotation of the illustrations occurs on each reduction, therefore two A4 sheets can be reproduced together.

## Sheet 3
- *Regarde les images et écris les mots*
  Look at the pictures and write the words
  – when access is given to the written word [AT4:1]
  – when the word is written from memory [AT4:2]
This indicates the knowledge of the French words for pictures given.

## Sheet 4
- *Joins les mots et les images*
  Join up the words and the pictures [AT3:1]
This indicates the ability to read individual words and to understand meanings.

## ◆ SET 2

### Format
- As before thick outlines mean pictures are to be affixed and thin outlines are for pictures to be drawn.
- However, double lines may now be used for writing phrases/sentences.
- The dialogue boxes are for either gluing pictures or for drawing.

### Use
These have a more extended use than Set 1 since they enable vocabulary to be linked to produce a phrase or sentence, for example, colour and animals/clothes, number and furniture, likes/dislikes and school subjects/hobbies. They can also be used as the basis for oral activities. Suggestions for the activities (below) will be less prescriptive than for Set 1 since they are open to a variety of uses by teachers. For example, there are several suitable rubrics for Sheet 1, and teachers should choose and insert the one they wish to use for a particular purpose.

### Activities and National Curriculum mapping
**Sheet 1** (three possible rubrics)
- *Regarde les images et copie la phrase*
  Look at the pictures and copy the sentence [AT4:2]
- *Regarde les images et complète la phrase*
  Look at the pictures and complete the sentence [AT4:2]
Here the sentence can have missing words which need to be supplied from the clues given in the pictures.
- *Regarde les images et écris la phrase*

Look at the pictures and write the sentence [AT4:3]
**Note:** before reaching the writing phase pupils can be encouraged to say the appropriate phrase/sentence [AT3:2] and, where the phrase is supplied, to read aloud.
**Sheet 2** (two possible rubrics)
• *Lis la phrase et dessine les images*
 Read the sentence and draw the pictures [AT3:2,3]
The pictures must be drawn in the appropriate order in relation to the elements of the sentence, e.g. *j'aime les chiens* needs heart then dog. The level achieved will depend upon the complexity of the sentence used.
• *Écoute la phrase et dessine les images*
 Listen to the sentence and draw the pictures [AT1:2]
As a follow-up activity pupils could then fill in the words.
**Sheet 3**
• *Complète les images et les phrases*
 Complete the pictures and the sentences [AT3:3, AT4:3]
This is a gap-filling activity where one of the pair of pictures and the other part of the phrase/sentence are supplied, and the pupils complete both elements from the clues given.
**Sheet 4** (three possible rubrics)
• *Écoute et dessine*
 Listen and draw            [AT1:2]
• *Écoute et écris les noms*
 Listen and write in the names
Pupils should listen to the teacher and then draw pictures or write names to show either **what** is liked/disliked or **who** likes/dislikes something.
• *Dessine dans la bonne case*
 Draw in the correct box
Using vocabulary from given topics, pupils can draw in their own likes/dislikes and this is then a basis for a speaking or writing activity [AT2:2,3, AT4:2,3].
**Sheets 5a and 5b** (four possible rubrics)
• *Regarde les images et lis le dialogue*
 Look at the pictures and read the dialogue [AT2:1]
This is a pairwork exercise with each pupil reading a part in the dialogue.
• *Complète les images et les phrases* (or *le dialogue*)
 Complete the pictures and the sentences (dialogue) [AT3:2]
As above, this is an information-gap exercise, where one picture and the other part of the dialogue are given with the pupil supplying the corresponding speech and picture.
• *Lis le dialogue (avec un partenaire) et dessine les images*
 Read the dialogue (aloud with a partner) and draw the pictures (5b)

Here the dialogue is given and the pupils show understanding by supplying the appropriate pictures [AT3:2].
• *Regarde les images et fais le dialogue*
 Look at the pictures and supply the dialogue (5a)
If this is done as a spoken exercise it is [AT2:3]; if it is written before being spoken in pairs it is [AT4:3].
**Note:** these could be used with directions and places in the town, questions and answers about likes and dislikes, finding out if someone has, or does, something, etc.

◆ **SET 3**

**Format**
Thick and thin outlines have the same significance as in Sets 1 and 2. Small boxes beneath pictures are for pupils to either indicate choice (✓ or ✗) or sequence, i.e. number.

**Use**
These sheets are intended as simple tests at the end of a module or topic to show pupils what they can do and to indicate to the teacher how much has been assimilated. Since some pupils may never be able to complete these exercises from memory, cues must always be available for those who need them. The tick-box sheet can be used for choices or for indicating the recognition of the sequence of items in a list.

**Activities and National Curriculum mapping**
**Sheet 1**
• *Regarde les images et écris les mots*
 Look at the pictures and write the words [AT4:2]
Here the pupil has to recall and correctly write the word.
**Sheet 2**
• *Lis les mots et dessine les images*
 Read the words and draw the pictures [AT3:1]
The pupil here indicates understanding of the written word.
**Sheet 3** (two possible rubrics)
• *Écoute et coche la bonne case*
 Listen and tick the right box [AT1:1,2]
Here the pupil chooses one of four items from spoken information, indicating understanding of the spoken word.
• *Écoute et numérote*
 Listen and show the order by writing a number in each box [AT1:1,2]
Here the pupils show they have recognized the sequence of items in a list, or the order of events, etc.

**Resources and activities**

| Game | Participation | | AT | Level |
|---|---|---|---|---|
| Bingo | individual | depending on level of difficulty of game | 1 | 1,2 |
| Pelmanism | pair/group | | 3 | 1 |
| Snap | pair | | 3 | 1 |
| Dominoes | group | | 3 | 1 |
| Noughts & crosses (OHT) | team | | 2 | 1 |
| Beetle | group | | 2 | 1 |
| Wordsearches | individual | finding words copying them | 3 | 1 |
| Hangman | pair | | 4 | 2 |
| Battleships | pair | | 1 | 1 |

National Curriculum mapping

# How to use the games

### Rationale

Games are a vital part of the learning process: they have an obvious motivating quality because they are fun, but they are also important because they are a way of using the newly-acquired foreign language in a real way; they are important, too, because they encourage pair and group work and so help in the socialization process which is important for pupils with Special Needs. They are often a time when pupils of all abilities are playing (working!) together with no problems of any kind. Games should not be underestimated; so long as they are well-prepared and well set-up, with pupils clear about ground rules, they allow topics to be practised using a range of skills and fulfilling the basic levels of all four attainment targets. They are particularly important because they encourage the use of memorized language which will eventually enable pupils to achieve more than just these basic levels of attainment.

### Making the most of the games

The **Extension** activities are suggestions for further exploiting the games. A game should, generally, be just the beginning of a series of activities and not simply an end in itself. For a start, the games take a fair amount of preparation, so it makes good sense to make full use of them. Secondly, once a game has motivated pupils, it is easy to build on reinforcing activities, without loss of interest or concentration.

### Winning

- The pupil who wins or completes a game/activity should call out *Ça y est!*
- Prizes are important to pupils where games are concerned. If teachers have the opportunity to go to France, they should collect things like illustrated wrapped sugar-cubes, hotel/restaurant visitors' cards, publicity sheets from tourist offices; also

large bags of French sweets are cheap and go a long way! But otherwise coloured stars, amusing inked stamps, stick-on badges, merits, etc. are fine.

## Bingo

This is played as an easy way to reinforce new vocabulary. The more restricted the vocabulary, the easier the level. The ready-made bingo cards are in appropriate shapes for the objects to be used for the game, e.g. food in a basket, etc. This helps pupils to focus on the set of vocabulary being used as well as helping them to categorize items.

Bingo is based on the original number game but with specialized blank templates for pupils to **draw** in (not write) items for themselves, as opposed to having ready-printed cards. The importance of this is that pupils are themselves deciding, within a given topic, what to include, e.g. any five animals from the ten learnt. In this way the game is self-differentiating and yet pupils all still have an equal chance of winning.

Once the items have been drawn onto the template, e.g. food in the basket, the teacher calls out random items (twice). Pupils circle those they have and, when all of their items are circled, they have won.

The winner then calls back the items in French so they can be checked before the prize is claimed. It is important that no English is spoken during the game – translation means disqualification!

### Extensions

1. e.g. animals in garden, also rooms/furniture, case/clothes, basket/shopping, etc.
- For the game the pupils draw in, say, five animals.
- Continue the game until three people have won.
- Then pupils can be asked to label their animals [AT4:1,2].
- Pupils may be required to exchange information about each other's animals in the garden [AT2:3].

- Pupils could be asked to write a simple sentence listing the animals in their garden [AT4:3].
- Pupils could colour in appropriate animals as you call out animals and colours [AT1:2].

In all of the written activities pupils can naturally differentiate the level because they may choose to work with or without cue words.

2. e.g. furniture and rooms in the house, also school timetable, row of shops and items for sale, etc.

Here the game is extended in the sense that later games become more and more complicated, requiring more and more understanding, memory, etc.

- **level 1** house outline, five unnamed rooms, and pupils simply put a piece of furniture in each of the five rectangles. They circle each piece as heard.
- **level 2** house outline, five named rooms, and pupils put a piece of furniture in each room. Now they need to listen for the correct room for the furniture they have drawn, i.e. if they have put a chair in the kitchen they can only count it if they hear *Une chaise dans la cuisine*. This encourages careful listening and is training for listening for specific detail.
- **level 3** as above, but any number of pieces of furniture are required to be drawn in each room, so that listening skills are extended.

Refer back to Extension 1. and you will see that any activity of that kind done with levels 2 or 3 will naturally be of a higher level of writing, reading or speaking.

## Snap

This requires one set of picture cards and a matching set of word cards, or a matching set of French and English word cards.

- Pair game matching French words with pictures, or French words with English equivalent.
- To avoid confusion and aid organization make each set of cards a different colour, i.e.
  - picture cards
  - French words
  - English equivalents
- For each game use French words and one of the other two sets.
- To play, each pupil holds one set of cards face down. In turn, players place their top card face up in front of them.
- If two cards match, the first person to recognize this and say *Ça y est!* claims the pair of cards and keeps them on the table.
- The game is over when either all of the cards have been won, or each set of cards has been gone through with no more matching pairs.
- The game is won by the player with the most pairs.

### Extensions (These activities can also be used with Pelmanism.)

- Pupils can be required to count in French the number of cards they have.
- They can inform partner/group of what they are

holding or five items that they are holding.
- They can copy into books any three pairs they are holding or which are laid out on the table by the winner.

## Pelmanism

- This makes use of the same sets of cards as snap, i.e. French words/pictures or French words/English equivalents.
- Cards are placed face down on the table.
- Players take turns in turning up one card of each colour and if they match they keep the pair.
- If they do not match, the cards are replaced face down, but they remain in the same place.
- The players should gradually memorize where cards are and this will help them to choose two that match and make a pair.
- When all of the cards have gone from the table, the winner is the player holding most pairs.

### Extensions (as for snap)

## Dominoes

This requires a set of cards with a picture and a word on each 'domino' – from the sample game supplied it will be apparent that, when making up the set, pictures and matching words need to be offset by one card, i.e. the word on the last card will match up with the picture on the first card.

- To ensure that the game can work out, follow the template and example carefully.
- Sets of cards need to be photocopied for groups to play. Copy each set onto different colour card, or number the reverse of sets, so that sets do not get mixed up.
- To play the game, the cards are all dealt out to three or four players. Because of the restricted vocabulary in a topic, there are not usually sufficient cards to play with a spare pile for players to use when they cannot go.
- One player starts by putting a card down. The next player needs to place a card to match and join up with either picture to word or word to picture, and so on, around the table.
- The player who cannot go misses a turn and play moves on to the next player.
- The winner is the one to use up all of the dealt cards first.
- A score can be kept of how many wins are scored by pupils during any one session (of, say, four games) and then a class prize can be awarded.

## Beetle

- This game is for up to six players (which can include a banker).
- Sets of pictures are needed (up to six within each set) and a die.
- The six chosen pictures correspond to a collectable group of items, e.g. set of clothes, food for a picnic, etc.

- The sets of cards need to be numbered 1–6 on the reverse, e.g. hats = 1, coats = 2, etc. (See example, page 57-8.)
- The pupils take it in turns to shake the die and ask for (or announce and take, if there is no banker) the item which matches the number thrown.
- If the number corresponds to an item already held by the player, that go is missed and the die goes on to the next player.
- 'Bankers cards', showing the six items and their die value, will help pupils ask for what they need.
- The game is won when one player has a complete set of pictures.

### Extensions
- When the game is over pupils can exchange information about what they are holding and also what they are lacking, thereby using negatives.
- Everyone in the group could be required to copy into their books the complete set of pictures and then label them.

## Noughts and crosses

This is a class team game using the OHP or the white/black board. This makes use of pictures only, and is therefore a memory recognition game and does not include reading. The idea is that the noughts and crosses frame starts off with pictures in its numbered squares. A member of a team (either O or X) picks a number and says in French what the picture is. If the answer is correct the picture is replaced by an O or an X as appropriate. The important thing about this game is that the team can be mixed-ability; **any** individual will be more interested in gaining a useful square, i.e. one which either helps towards a line or blocks a line from the other team, than in the pictures themselves, so will **risk** giving an uncertain word, rather than playing safe with a familiar word, since there is a definite aim in the choice. Too often SEN pupils do not take risks.

### Extensions
- This can become a reading game. Pupils show understanding by placing the correct picture with the word/caption, and thus gaining their O or X.
- Complications can be added by having complex pictures or phrases, e.g. like/dislike and item, number and object.

## Hangman

This is basically a spelling game played in pairs or teams, but again is self-differentiating, as no-one will choose an unknown word. There is always the risk here that a pupil may spell a word incorrectly, but this is a natural problem in life and hopefully one pupil might pick up the mistake, which will make it part of the learning process.

## Wordsearch

Initially words should go horizontally and vertically only. The puzzle may be complicated by using diagonals later, but the words should **never** be entered backwards.

For the puzzle, either the French words that are hidden can be given, or the words and pictures, or just the pictures. The latter is the most difficult since the pupil needs to think what the word is first, then find it.

### Extensions
- If just the words are given, when the puzzle is completed a picture could be drawn for each to show comprehension.
- A written task could follow the puzzle, with the word being copied under each picture.
In both cases, learning and spelling are being reinforced.

Blank wordsearches can also be given to pupils to make up their own puzzles. This is not only creative (important for the National Curriculum), but it is also a meaningful task, since pupils can then swap puzzles.

## Battleships

The basic game uses a grid with numbers across the top and letters down one side. Pupils put given items, e.g. school subjects, into squares and partners find out where each other's vocabulary is hidden by asking 'A4? B3?' etc. Correct guesses are scored as hits, and marked off by each player.

### Extension
- The game is much more communicative, however, if the grids combine two elements of a final sentence where each player has to complete the other's sentences, e.g. names across the top, animals down the side.
- Players tick their choice of boxes. The players take turns asking, *Est-ce que Paul a un lapin?* etc. If that square has been ticked the response is *'oui'* and this is scored as a hit.

## Kim's game

This requires a tray, some objects and a cloth to cover the tray. It can be either a simple memory game where pupils, in teams or individually, recall as many of the objects as possible, or, while the tray is covered an object can be removed and then pupils have to name the missing object.

*LE FRANÇAIS, C'EST FACILE!*

# Blank worksheets and examples

**Module** _____ **Topic** _____

Copie les mots et les images
----------------------------------------------------------------

*LE FRANÇAIS, C'EST FACILE!*

**Module** _____|_____ **Topic** _____3_____

Copie les mots et les images _____

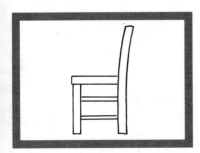  la chaise _____

_____

  la salle de classe

_____

  le tableau _____

_____

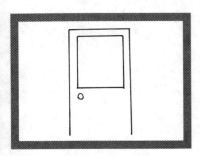  la porte _____

_____

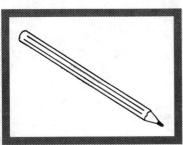  le crayon _____

_____

• • • • • • • • • • • • • • • • • • • • • • • • • • • • • • • • •

**Module** _____ **Topic** _____

Lis les mots et dessine les images

---

_____

_____

_____

_____

_____

Lis les mots et dessine les images

*LE FRANÇAIS, C'EST FACILE!*

**Module** _____ I _____ **Topic** _____ 3 _____

Lis les mots et dessine les images _____

le livre

la table

le crayon

le tableau

la règle

**Module** _____ **Topic** _____

Regarde les images et écris les mots _____

*LE FRANÇAIS, C'EST FACILE!*

**Module** _____2_____ **Topic** _____4_____

Regarde les images et écris les mots

*LE FRANÇAIS, C'EST FACILE!*

**Module** _____ **Topic** _____

<u>Joins les mots et les images</u>

*LE FRANÇAIS, C'EST FACILE!*

**Module** _____3_____    **Topic** _____1_____

Joins les mots et les images _____

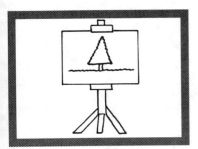                    la musique

                    les maths

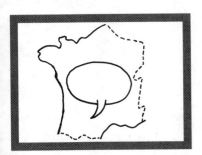                    le sport

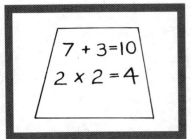                    L'art

                    le francais

**Module** _____ **Topic** _____

------------------------------------------------------------------

*LE FRANÇAIS, C'EST FACILE!*

**Module** _____3_____    **Topic** _____2_____

Regarde les images et complète la phrase.

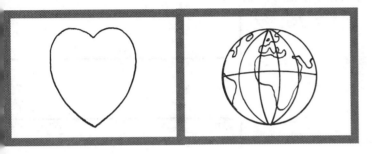   la géographie

   Je n'aime pas

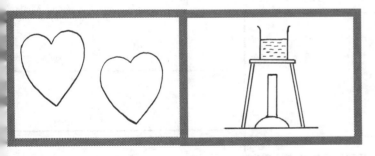   J'adore

   l'informatique

**Module**_____ **Topic**_____

-------------------------------------------------------------------------

**Module** _____5_____  **Topic** _____3_____

Lis la phrase et dessine les images

Je n'aime pas

le fromage

J'adore

le chocolat

Je déteste

le café

Je préfère

la glace

**Module**_____ **Topic**_____

Complète les images et les phrases _____

_____

_____

_____

_____

_____

_____

_____

_____

*LE FRANÇAIS, C'EST FACILE!*

**Module** _____ 4 _____  **Topic** _____ 6 _____

Complète les images et les phrases _____

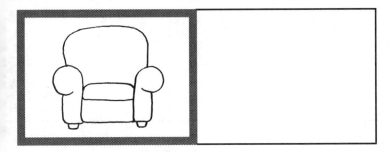

Il y a _____

dans le salon _____

Il y a un lit _____

dans _____

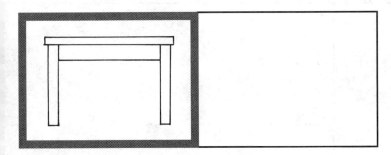

_____

dans la salle à manger

_____ un chien

dans _____

● ● ● ● ● ● ● ● ● ● ● ● ● ● ● ● ● ● ● ● ● ● ● ● ● ● ● ● ● ● ●

**Module**_____ **Topic**_____

---

|  |  |  |  |
|---|---|---|---|
|  |  |  |  |
|  |  |  |  |

|  |  |
|---|---|
|  |  |
|  |  |

*LE FRANÇAIS, C'EST FACILE!*

**Module** _____ 6 _____  **Topic** _____ 4 _____

Écoute et écris les noms _____

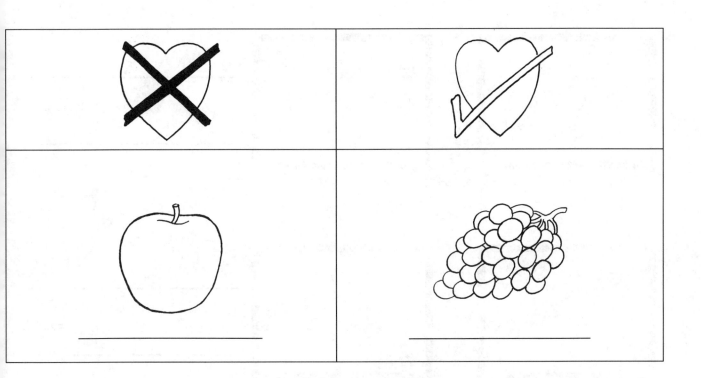

## Module_____ Topic_____

-----------------------------------------------------------------------

*LE FRANÇAIS, C'EST FACILE!*

**Module** _____3_____ **Topic** _____5_____

## Regarde les images et fais le dialogue

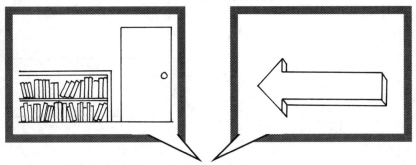

Où est la bibliothèque ?

_____

Où est le laboratoire ?

_____

_____ la cour ?

_____

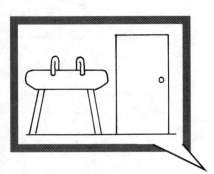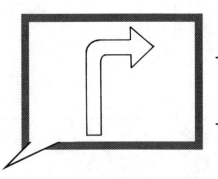

_____ ?

_____

**Module**_____ **Topic**_____

--------------------------------------------------------------------

*LE FRANÇAIS, C'EST FACILE!*

**Module** _____5_____     **Topic** _____5_____

Lis le dialogue (avec un partenaire) et dessine les images

C'est combien,
la pomme ?

Deux francs

C'est combien,
le sandwich ?

Sept francs

Le stylo,
c'est combien ?

C'est 13 francs

C'est combien,
la bouteille de vin ?

C'est 30 francs

**Module**_____ **Topic**_____

Regarde les images et écris les mots _____

*LE FRANÇAIS, C'EST FACILE!*

**Module** ___9___     **Topic** ___3___

Regarde les images et écris les mots

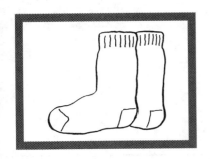  

_____  _____  _____

 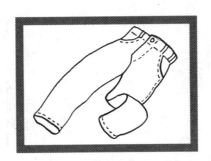 

_____  _____  _____

 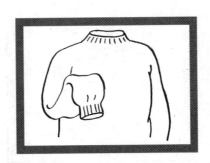 

_____  _____  _____

**Module**_____ **Topic**_____

<u>Lis les mots et dessine les images</u>

*LE FRANÇAIS, C'EST FACILE!*

**Module** _____8_____ **Topic** _____3_____

Lis les mots et dessine les images _____

| | | |
|---|---|---|
| les dents | les oreilles | le football |
| le cyclisme | le tennis | le pied |
| la main | le nez | l'équitation |

**Module**_____ **Topic**_____

--------------------------------------------------------------------------------

*LE FRANÇAIS, C'EST FACILE!*

**Module** _____7_____    **Topic** _____4_____

Écoute et coche la bonne case

# Blank activity and game templates

## Games templates

Template    1     Pelmanism/Snap/Beetle
              2     Dominoes
              3a    Noughts and crosses (grid)
              3b    Noughts and crosses
              4a    Wordsearch (10 x 10)
              4b    Wordsearch (14 x 14)
              5a    Battleships (A–E, 1–5)
              5b    Battleships (blank for pictures)

Example    1     Pelmanism/Snap
             2     Beetle
             3     Dominoes
             4     Wordsearch
             5     Battleships

## Additional activity/resource templates

Template    6     ID cards
              7     Speech bubbles
              8     Clock
              9     Likes/dislikes
             10    Survey sheet
             11    Map of La Manche
         12a–c  Shop names
         13a,b  Days of the week
             14    Girls' names and boys' names
         15a,b  Numbers
             16    Alphabet
             17    Map of France with town names

# Pelmanism/Snap/Beetle

# Dominoes

**Template 3a**

**Noughts and crosses**

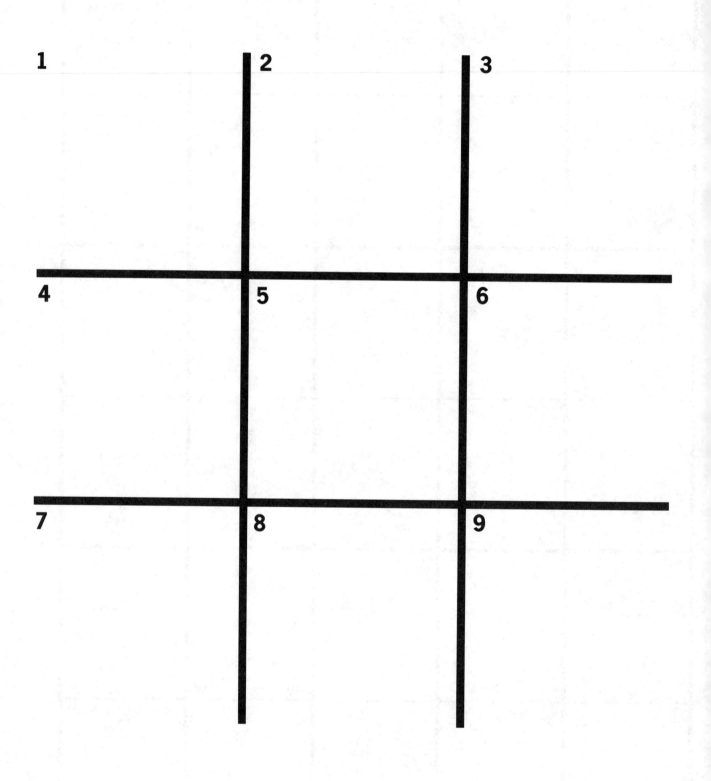

# Noughts and crosses

O X

O X

O X X

O O X

# Wordsearch 10 X 10

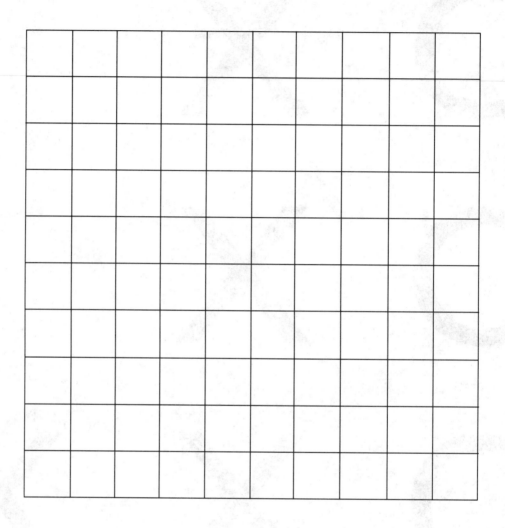

# Wordsearch 14 X 14

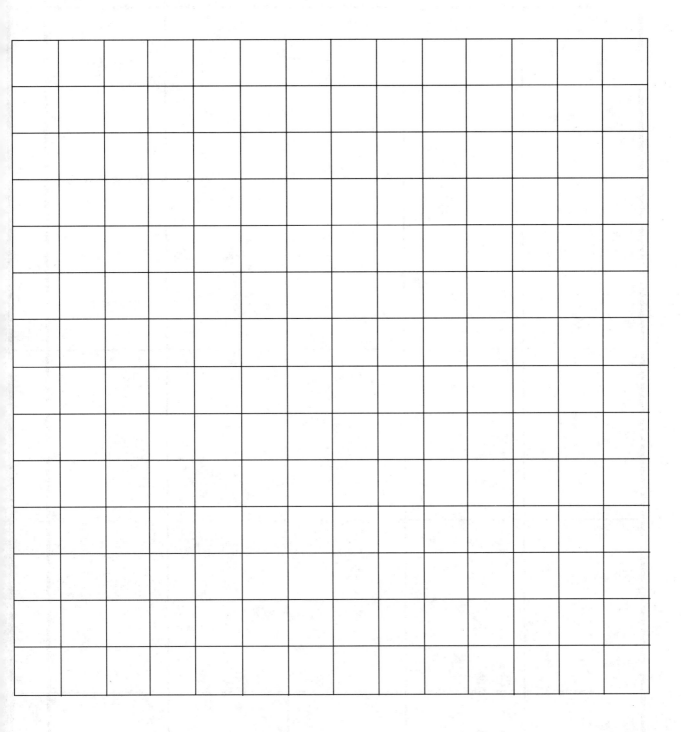

**Template 5a**

# Battleships

|  | 5 | 4 | 3 | 2 | 1 |
|---|---|---|---|---|---|
| A |  |  |  |  |  |
| B |  |  |  |  |  |
| C |  |  |  |  |  |
| D |  |  |  |  |  |
| E |  |  |  |  |  |

# Battleships

**Example 1**

## Pelmanism/Snap
These need sets of picture and corresponding word cards, preferably on different coloured card.

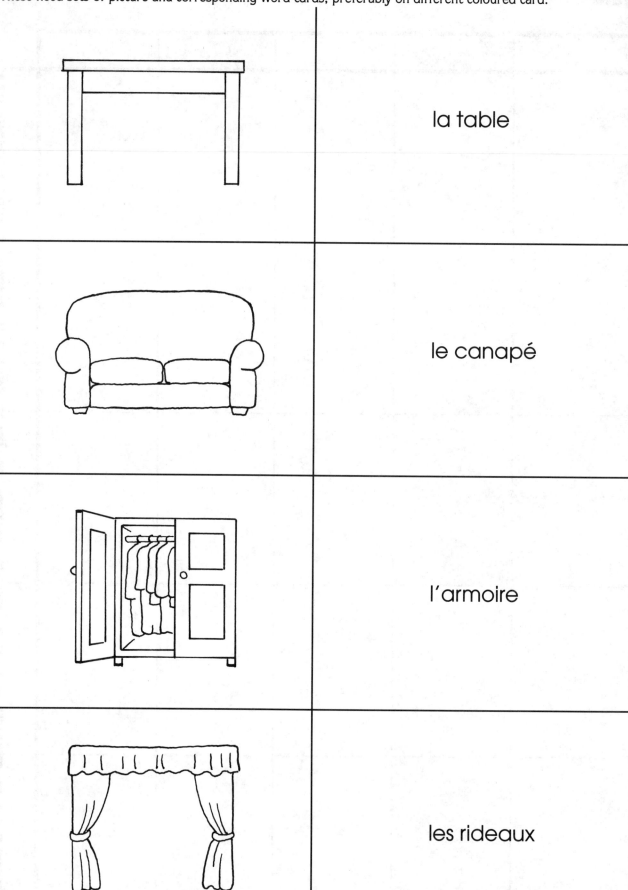

| | |
|---|---|
| | la table |
| | le canapé |
| | l'armoire |
| | les rideaux |

**Example 2**

# Beetle

This needs sets of up to six pictures, numbered on the reverse, and a die. A 'banker's card', showing the six items and their die value, will help pupils ask for what they need.

| | |
|---|---|
| 1 = le chapeau | |
| 2 = le pull | |
| 3 = le jean | |
| 4 = les chaussettes | |
| 5 = les chaussures | |

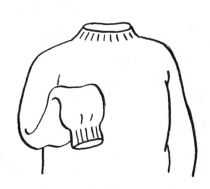

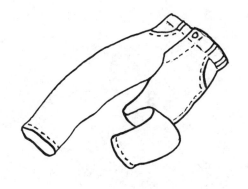

2

1

4

3

5

Example 3

# Dominoes

| | | | | |
|---|---|---|---|---|
| la patinoire | le marché | la ville | le théâtre | le cinéma |
| la maison | le supermarché | l'école | le terrain de football | le café |
| la disco | la piscine | le parc | le tabac | le port |

*LE FRANÇAIS, C'EST FACILE!*

59

**Example 4**

# Wordsearch 10 X 10

| a | r | u | g | b | y | c | b | c | d |
|---|---|---|---|---|---|---|---|---|---|
| é | g | f | k | p | g | i | z | t | r |
| s | b | a | d | m | i | n | t | o | n |
| p | a | s | m | l | j | é | e | b | d |
| o | s | j | v | w | n | m | n | o | c |
| r | k | j | o | p | a | a | n | h | i |
| t | é | l | é | v | i | s | i | o | n |
| s | t | u | m | x | a | e | s | y | s |
| l | j | a | r | d | i | n | a | g | e |
| f | o | o | t | b | a | l | l | t | b |

basket
badminton
tennis
télévision
sports
jardinage
football
rugby
cinéma

Example 5

# Battleships

| un hamster | un chat | une souris | un chien | un poisson rouge | |
|---|---|---|---|---|---|
| | | | | | Philippe |
| | | | | | Thomas |
| | | | | | Natalie |
| | | | | | Sandrine |
| | | | | | Nicolas |

# ID cards

nom......................... prénom.................
âge.................
adresse.................................................
...............................................................

nom......................... prénom.................
âge.................
adresse.................................................
...............................................................

*LE FRANÇAIS, C'EST FACILE!*

# Speech bubbles

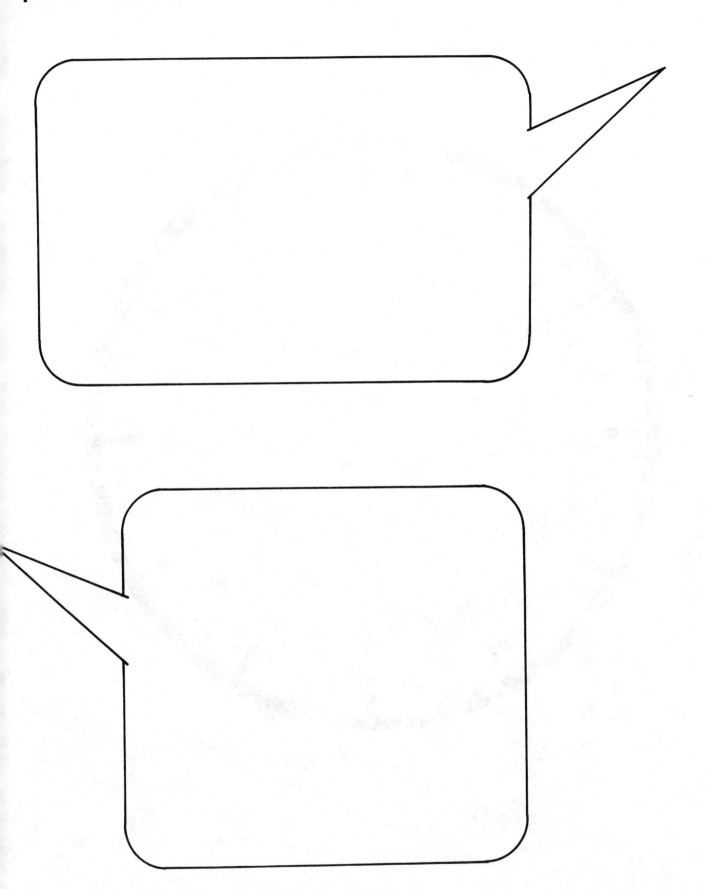

# Clock

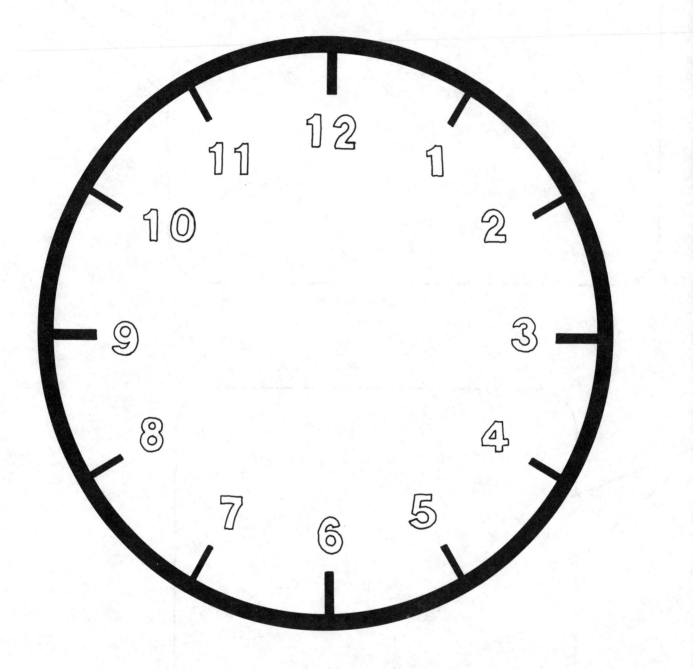

## Likes/dislikes

# J'AIME

# JE N'AIME PAS

**Template 10**

# Survey sheet

|  |  |  |  |  |  |
|--|--|--|--|--|--|
|  |  |  |  |  |  |
|  |  |  |  |  |  |
|  |  |  |  |  |  |
|  |  |  |  |  |  |
|  |  |  |  |  |  |
|  |  |  |  |  |  |
|  |  |  |  |  |  |
|  |  |  |  |  |  |
|  |  |  |  |  |  |
|  |  |  |  |  |  |
|  |  |  |  |  |  |
|  |  |  |  |  |  |
|  |  |  |  |  |  |

*LE FRANÇAIS, C'EST FACILE!*

**Example 10**

# Survey sheet

| | 🎨 | 🏭 | 🌐 | 💻 | 🎵 | 🗺️ |
|---|---|---|---|---|---|---|
| Donna | | | | | | |
| Kerry | | | | | | |
| Alan | | | | | | |
| Shane | | | | | | |
| | | | | | | |
| | | | | | | |
| | | | | | | |
| | | | | | | |
| | | | | | | |
| | | | | | | |
| | | | | | | |
| | | | | | | |
| | | | | | | |

**La Manche – The English Channel**

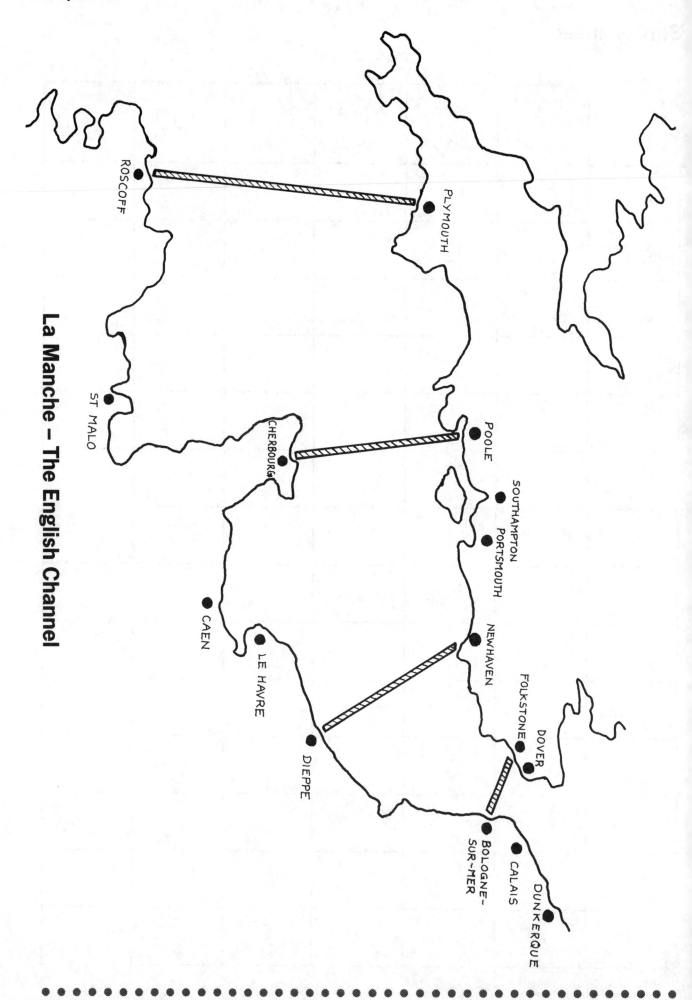

ROSCOFF

PLYMOUTH

ST MALO

CHERBOURG

POOLE

SOUTHAMPTON

PORTSMOUTH

CAEN

LE HAVRE

NEWHAVEN

FOLKSTONE

DOVER

DIEPPE

BOLOGNE-SUR-MER

CALAIS

DUNKERQUE

# Shop names

## la boucherie

## la boulangerie

## la charcuterie

## l'épicerie

**Shop names**

# l'alimentation

# l'hypermarché

# le magasin

# Shop names

le marché

le supermarché

le tabac

**Days of the week**

# lundi

# mardi

# mercredi

# jeudi

# Days of the week

vendredi

samedi

dimanche

| Some French girls' names | Some French boys' names |
| --- | --- |
| Annick | Arnaud |
| Elodie | Christian |
| Farida | Daniel |
| Florence | Eric |
| Isabelle | Hussein |
| Karine | Jean-Luc |
| Madeleine | Laurent |
| Marilyne | Ludovic |
| Nabila | Matthieu |
| Natalie | Nicolas |
| Sandrine | Omar |
| Sylvie | Philippe |
| Valérie | Thierry |
| Yasmine | Thomas |

## Numbers 1–31

| | | | |
|---|---|---|---|
| 0 | zéro | 16 | seize |
| 1 | un | 17 | dix-sept |
| 2 | deux | 18 | dix-huit |
| 3 | trois | 19 | dix-neuf |
| 4 | quatre | 20 | vingt |
| 5 | cinq | 21 | vingt et un |
| 6 | six | 22 | vingt-deux |
| 7 | sept | 23 | vingt-trois |
| 8 | huit | 24 | vingt-quatre |
| 9 | neuf | 25 | vingt-cinq |
| 10 | dix | 26 | vingt-six |
| 11 | onze | 27 | vingt-sept |
| 12 | douze | 28 | vingt-huit |
| 13 | treize | 29 | vingt-neuf |
| 14 | quatorze | 30 | trente |
| 15 | quinze | 31 | trente et un |

# Numbers 32–100

| | | |
|---|---|---|
| 32 trente-deux | 55 cinquante-cinq | 78 soixante-dix-huit |
| 33 trente-trois | 56 cinquante-six | 79 soixante-dix-neuf |
| 34 trente-quatre | 57 cinquante-sept | 80 quatre-vingts |
| 35 trente-cinq | 58 cinquante-huit | 81 quatre-vingt-un |
| 36 trente-six | 59 cinquante-neuf | 82 quatre-vingt-deux |
| 37 trente-sept | 60 soixante | 83 quatre-vingt-trois |
| 38 trente-huit | 61 soixante et un | 84 quatre-vingt-quatre |
| 39 trente-neuf | 62 soixante-deux | 85 quatre-vingt-cinq |
| 40 quarante | 63 soixante-trois | 86 quatre-vingt-six |
| 41 quarante et un | 64 soixante-quatre | 87 quatre-vingt-sept |
| 42 quarante-deux | 65 soixante-cinq | 88 quatre-vingt-huit |
| 43 quarante-trois | 66 soixante-six | 89 quatre-vingt-neuf |
| 44 quarante-quatre | 67 soixante-sept | 90 quatre-vingt-dix |
| 45 quarante-cinq | 68 soixante-huit | 91 quatre-vingt-onze |
| 46 quarante-six | 69 soixante-neuf | 92 quatre-vingt-douze |
| 47 quarante-sept | 70 soixante-dix | 93 quatre-vingt-treize |
| 48 quarante-huit | 71 soixante et onze | 94 quatre-vingt-quatorze |
| 49 quarante-neuf | 72 soixante-douze | 95 quatre-vingt-quinze |
| 50 cinquante | 73 soixante-treize | 96 quatre-vingt-seize |
| 51 cinquante et un | 74 soixante-quatorze | 97 quatre-vingt-dix-sept |
| 52 cinquante-deux | 75 soixante-quinze | 98 quatre-vingt-dix-huit |
| 53 cinquante-trois | 76 soixante-seize | 99 quatre-vingt-dix-neuf |
| 54 cinquante-quatre | 77 soixante-dix-sept | 100 cent |

# Alphabet

Aa

Bb

Cc

Dd

Ee

Ff

Gg

Hh

Ii

Jj

Kk

Ll

Mm

Nn

Oo

Pp

Qq

Rr

Ss

Tt

Uu

Vv

Ww

Xx

Yy

Zz

# Map of France

# L'EMPLOI DU TEMPS

**Bingo B4**

| EMPLOI DU TEMPS | |
|---|---|
| | LUNDI |
| | MARDI |
| | MERCREDI |
| | JEUDI |
| | VENDREDI |

*LE FRANÇAIS, C'EST FACILE!*

| JOUR / LEÇON | 1 | 2 | 3 | 4 |
|---|---|---|---|---|
| LUNDI | | | | |
| MARDI | | | | |
| MERCREDI | | | | |
| JEUDI | | | | |
| VENDREDI | | | | |

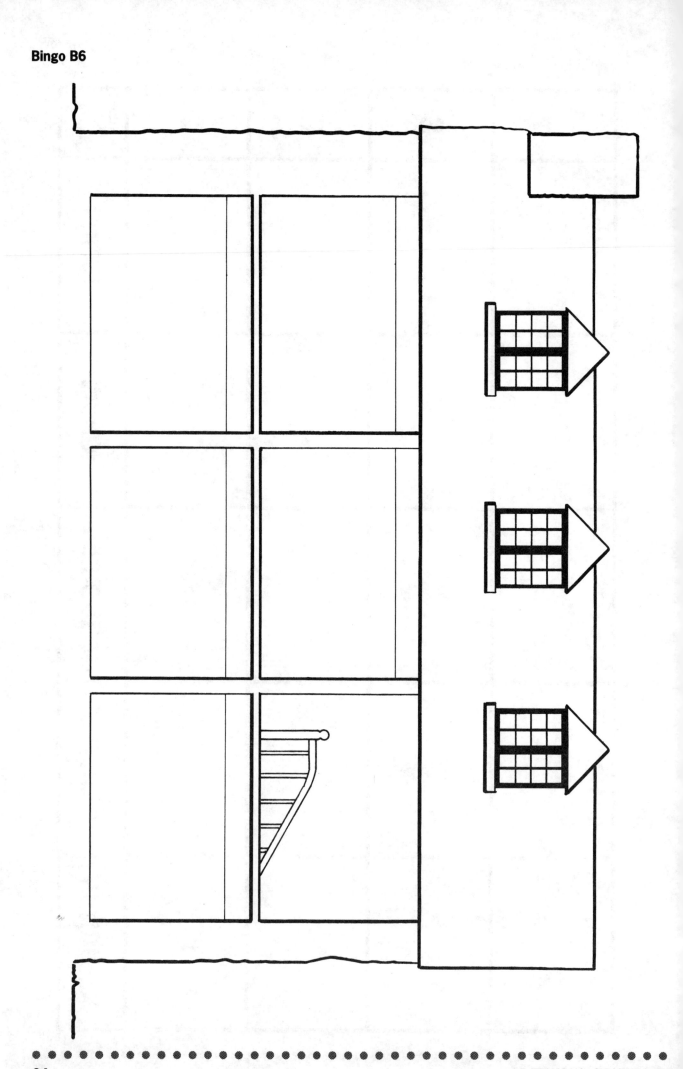

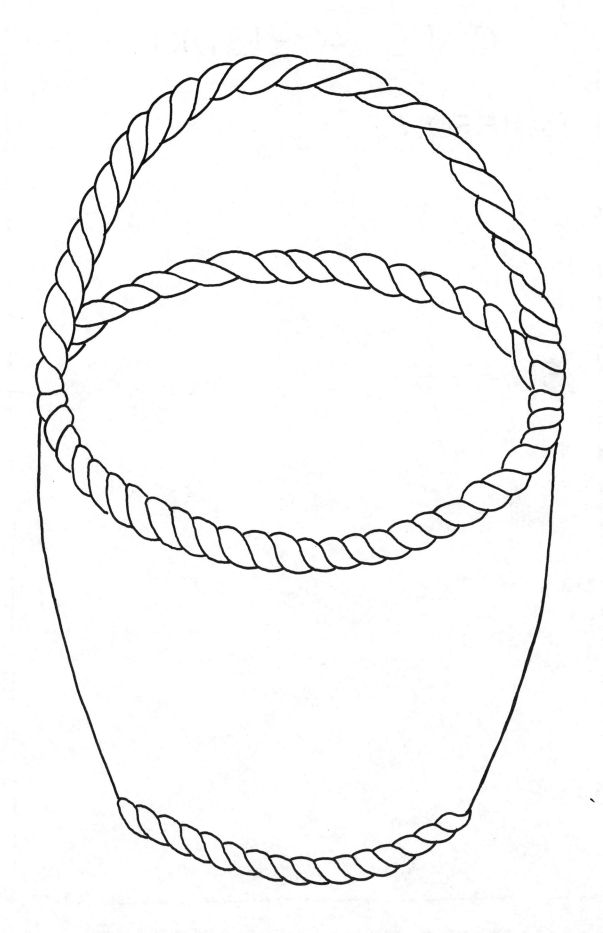

# CAFÉ AVEL MOR

## BOISSONS

## SNACKS

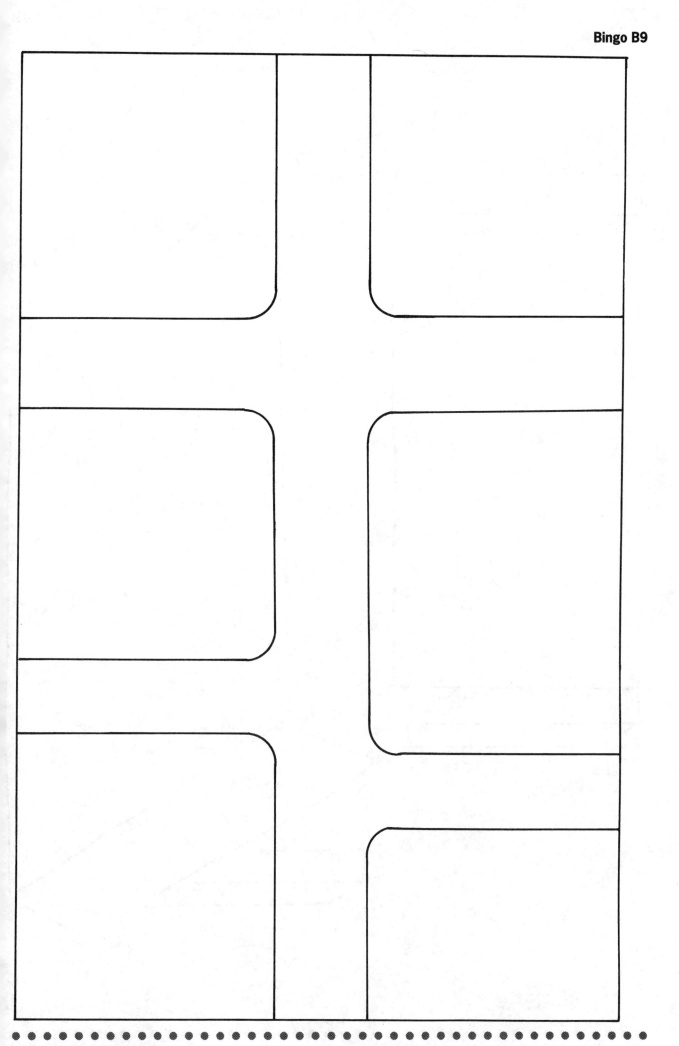

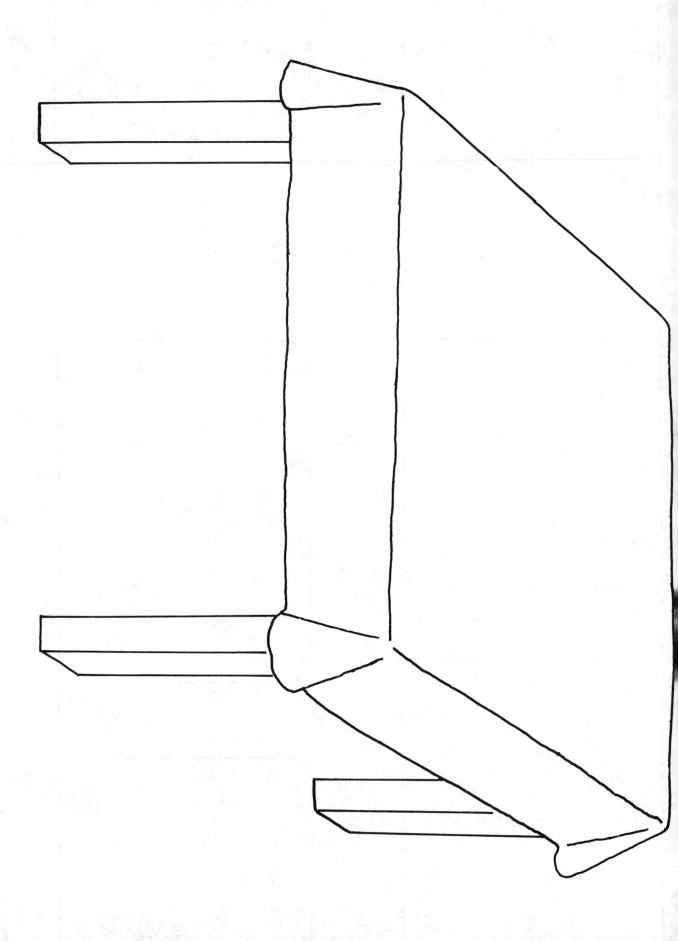

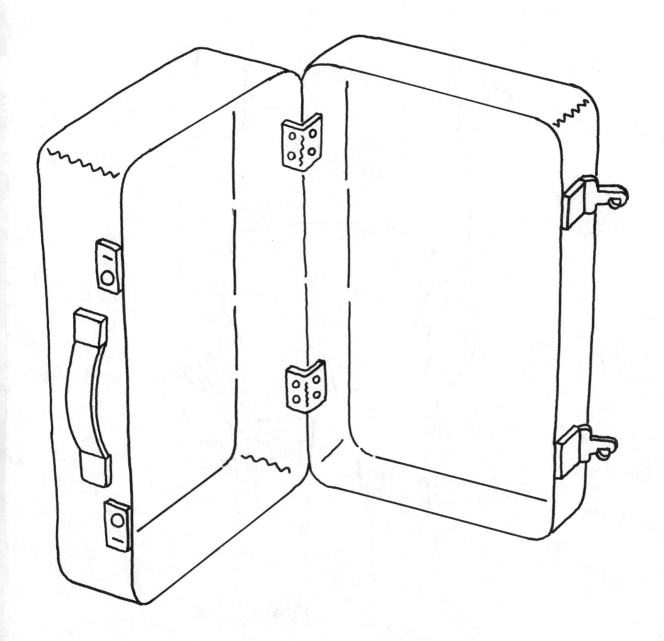

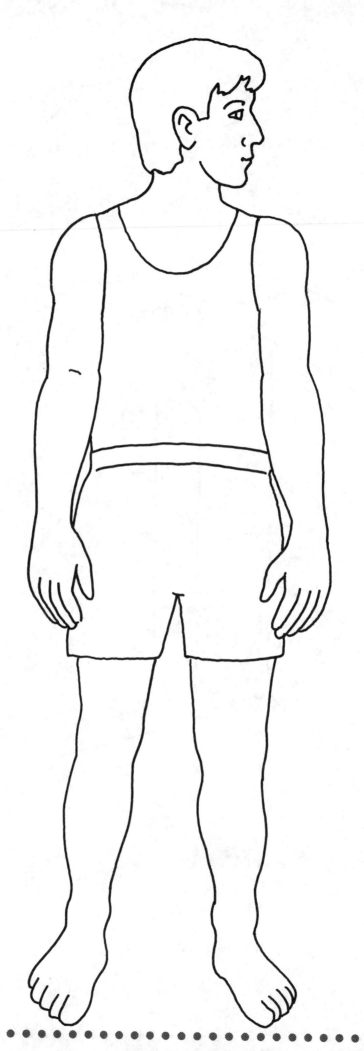

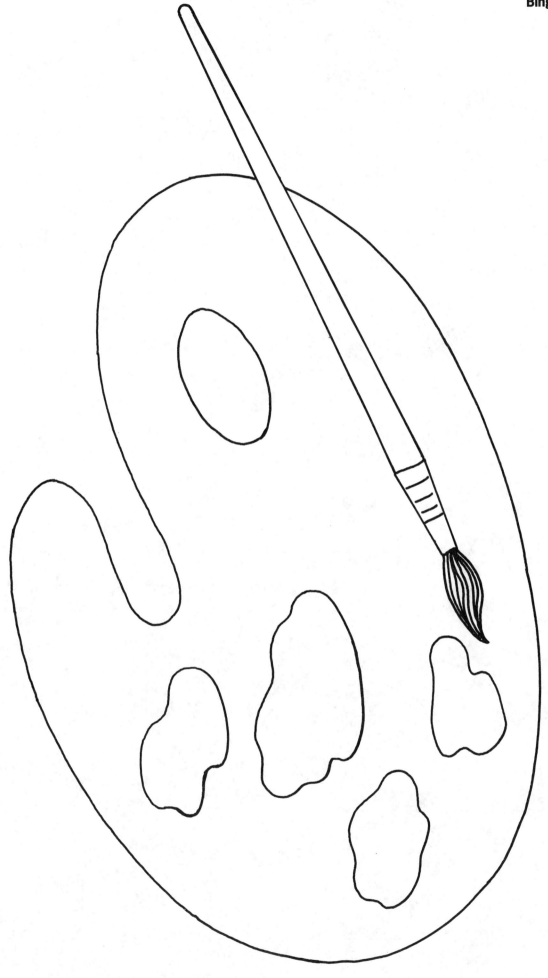

# MODULE 1 Here I am

## Timescale
1 term

## Areas of experience
A   B

## Topics / Communicative objectives

| Topics | Communicative objectives |
|---|---|
| (i) Greetings | Initiating and responding to simple greetings |
| (ii) Introducing oneself | Asking for and giving name |
| (iii) Classroom objects | Understanding and naming the objects in the classroom |
| (iv) Getting involved | Responding to instructions in the foreign language classroom |
| (v) Numbers and alphabet | Understanding and using numbers 0–31 and the alphabet |
| (vi) Personal details | Exchanging information about age and where I live |

## Assignments
Designing and making classroom signs

Designing and compiling a phrase book

Making ID card

## Programme of study (part 1): Examples
Communicating in the target language
– ask and answer questions

Understanding and responding
– follow clear directions and instructions

Developing language-learning skills
– learn phrases by heart

## Cross-curricular opportunities

| | |
|---|---|
| Number practice | } Maths |
| Counting and simple calculations | |
| Designing and making (assignments) | Design and Technology Information technology |
| Role play and pairwork | PSE |

## Opportunities for assessment

| | |
|---|---|
| Respond to flashcards/ play games | AT1:1; AT2:1,2 |
| Understand other people giving name | AT1:1 |
| Ask/answer questions about name/age | AT1:1; AT2:1,2 |
| Play *Simon dit* | AT1:1,2 |
| Say own name/cue card name | AT2:1 |
| Match words to objects/pictures | AT3:1 |
| Label pictures/objects | AT4:1 |

# Module 1 Here I am
# Topic (i) Greetings

| | |
|---|---|
| **Topic**<br>(i) Greetings | **Communicative objective**<br>Initiating and responding to simple greetings |

**Linguistic objectives (examples)**

*Bonjour*

*Ça va*

*Bien*

*Oui*

*Non*

*Et toi?*

*Merci*

*Au revoir*

*À bientôt*

**Activities**

- Begin by greeting pupils and encouraging them to respond
- Reinforce meanings with flashcards
- Match words and pictures
- Pairwork – role play
- Copy-writing
- Song

**Resources**

- Greetings flashcards
- Cue cards
- Sets of pictures/cue cards for building sentences

- Song cassette

Few resources are needed here – these introductory lessons rely heavily on gesture, mime and role play

**Assignments**

Make up and perform a greetings sketch

Start to compile a phrase book

*LE FRANÇAIS, C'EST FACILE!*

# Module 1 Here I am

# Topic (ii) Introducing oneself

**Topic**
(ii) Introducing oneself

**Communicative objective**
Asking for and giving name

**Linguistic objectives (examples)**

*Comment t'appelles-tu?*
*tu t'appelles?*

*Je m'appelle . . .*

*Et toi?*

**Activities**
- Simple teacher-led question and answer
- Pairs/groups as above
- Pupils take French name cards and say who they are
- Pupils take picture cards and say who they are
- Copying words and phrases
- IT opportunity

**Resources**
- Name cards, template 15

- Pictures of famous people (of interest to teenagers!)

**Assignments**
Working towards ID card and playlet

# Module 1 Here I am

# Topic (iii) Classroom objects

● ● ● ● ● ● ● ● ● ● ● ● ● ● ● ● ● ● ● ● ● ● ● ● ● ● ● ● ● ● ● ● ● ● ● ● ● ● ●

## Topic
(iii) Classroom objects

## Communicative objective
Understanding and naming the objects in the classroom

## Linguistic objectives (examples)

| | |
|---|---|
| la chaise | C'est(?) . . . |
| la fenêtre | Oui |
| le mur | Non |
| la porte | Tu as . . .? |
| la salle de classe | J'ai |
| la table | sur |
| le tableau | dans |
| le cahier | Il y a . . . |
| le cartable | Indiquez . . . |
| le crayon | Touchez . . . |
| le feutre* | Je voudrais . . . |
| la gomme | Voilà |
| le livre | |
| le papier | |
| la règle | |
| le stylo* | |

* use most relevant
to class

## Activities
- After presentation pupils point to, touch, bring out objects
- Play *Simon dit* with the above
- Snap and Pelmanism to match words and pictures
- True/false games
- Kim's game
- Classroom objects wordsearch
- Make up your own wordsearch
- Copy-writing to label pictures and objects
- Song

## Resources
- Worksheets Set 1, 1–4
- Classroom object flashcards
- Small images to make wordsearch
- Snap and Pelmanism cards
- Bingo, template B1
- Noughts and crosses, templates 3a and 3b for OHP
- Ready-made wordsearch, template 4a or 4b
- Blank wordsearch to make up, template 4a

- Card for pupils to make labels
- Classroom objects
- Cue cards
- Song cassette

## Assignments
Making classroom signs

Continuing phrase book

● ● ● ● ● ● ● ● ● ● ● ● ● ● ● ● ● ● ● ● ● ● ● ● ● ● ● ● ● ● ● ● ● ● ● ● ● ● ●

*LE FRANÇAIS, C'EST FACILE!*

# Module 1 Here I am

# Topic (iv) Getting involved

●●●●●●●●●●●●●●●●●●●●●●●●●●●●●●●●●●●●●●●●●●●●

## Topic
(iv) Getting involved

## Communicative objective
Responding to instructions in the foreign language classroom

## Linguistic objectives (examples)
*Asseyez-vous/Assieds-toi*

*Cherchez/Cherche*

*Copiez/Copie*

*Dessinez/Dessine*

*Écoutez/Écoute*

*Écrivez/Écris*

*Fermez/Ferme*

*Jouez/Joue*

*Levez-vous/Lève-toi*

*Montrez/Montre*

*Ouvrez/Ouvre*

*Prenez/Prends*

*Regardez/Regarde*

*Répétez/Répète*

*Répondez/Réponds*

*Venez/Viens ici*

This is a long list, but remember it is receptive rather than productive vocabulary

## Activities
- After presentation use gestures and mimes to reinforce meaning
- Play *Simon dit*
- Matching words to symbols

**Note:** nothing needs to be written here

## Resources
- Flashcards      classroom commands
  classroom objects
- Cue cards      classroom commands
  classroom objects

- Classroom objects

## Assignments
Making own cue cards with words and symbols to make classroom display for daily use

●●●●●●●●●●●●●●●●●●●●●●●●●●●●●●●●●●●●●●●●●●●●

# Module 1 Here I am

# Topic (v) Numbers and alphabet

**Topic**
(v) Numbers and alphabet

**Communicative objective**
Understanding and using numbers 0–31 and the alphabet

**Linguistic objectives (examples)**
Numbers 0–31

*Combien?*

Alphabet

Classroom objects from topic (iii)

**Activities**
- Counting objects
- Worksheets Set 2, 1 and 2
- Identify numbers in a sequence
- Sums
- How many times did I say?
- Matching activities
- Bingo
- Dominoes
- Singing numbers to raps/tunes
- Alphabet games – what comes next?
                        what is missing?
- Spelling own name
- Fill in missing letter
- Two songs

**Resources**
- Worksheets Set 2, 1 and 2
- Classroom object flashcards
- Song cassette
- Dominoes, template 2 for digits/words – numbers
- Number cards, template 15a

- Number cards, digits and words, for matching alphabet frieze
- Song cassette

**Assignments**
Alphabet/number rap

For classroom display link number cue cards in visual form with different numbers of classroom objects

# Module 1 Here I am

# Topic (vi) Personal details

## Topic
(vi) Personal details

## Communicative objective
Exchanging information about age and where I live

## Linguistic objectives (examples)

*Quel âge as-tu?*

*Tu as quel âge?*

*J'ai . . . ans*

*Où habites-tu?*

*Tu habites où?*

*J'habite à . . .*

Numbers

Additional receptive vocabulary:

*nom*

*prénom*

*âge*

*adresse*

## Activities
After presentation:

- Pairwork
- Simulations using mixture of name/age/town cards
- Building up sentences
- Filling out ID card
- Copy-writing of new phrases
- Worksheet Set 3, 2 can be used to practise numbers. Given words, pupils can write the digits.

## Resources
- Worksheet Set 3, 2
- Name/age (number)/town cards
- Outline ID card, template 6

- Blank cassettes

## Assignments
Making an ID card

Making up a dialogue and performing/recording it

**Note:** remember, from now on, to always develop the phrase book

# Module 1: Here I am

●●●●●●●●●●●●●●●●●●●●●●●●●●●●●●●●●●●●●●●●●●

## General notes on the module

- This introductory module is not typical of the rest of the course.
- Its role is to introduce the pupils to the language needed to participate in later activities, to introduce the activities and games themselves, to show how mime and gesture help understanding and to get the pupils using French as quickly as possible.
- Details given in this module for the presentation of new vocabulary, etc. will not be repeated in later modules, where teaching notes will begin after the initial presentation.

## 1(i) Greetings

- Begin immediately by saying *Bonjour* and shaking hands with as many pupils as possible.
- Pupils will gradually start to respond quite naturally.
- Now encourage this.
- Words and phrases should now be said to elicit all kinds of repetition by class, group and individual.
- Also encourage repetition in different ways, e.g. quietly, loudly, angrily, sadly, etc. This will help to vary the very important stage of repetition, which can otherwise become boring.
- Pupils can now work in pairs/groups on greetings.
- No writing need necessarily be done at this stage, although copy-writing after a reading or aural exercise building up utterances often helps reinforcement and memory.

### Assignment

- Pupils should perform a short sketch with a small group greeting each other, shaking hands, saying *'Ça va?'* and then taking their leave.
- This greetings sketch is working towards the final dialogue of the module.
- The phrase book is important since it encourages careful copy-writing and will encourage dictionary skills later.

## 1(ii) Introducing oneself

- This extends Topic 1(i) by just a few phrases.
- Follow the same kind of presentation initially.
- Some pictures of famous (to today's teenagers, remember) people will add interest – pupils can choose to be somebody else or be given a person to be.

**Note:** we are not here introducing *Il/Elle s'appelle* – at this stage we want nothing to confuse the giving of clear information about oneself.

- Games can be played with flashcards where the picture is only gradually revealed.
- The French name cards will serve two purposes – to introduce the pupils to French names and to give an activity similar to the one above.

  **Note:** it is advisable to copy the names onto card, colour-coded, for boys/girls so that when pupils pick a card and pretend to be that person, they get the correct gender.

- Listening – all courses have young people greeting each other in early units, so any cassettes available to you will be useful here for pupils to recognize names and voices.

### Assignment

There is no complete assignment in this small topic but pupils can add new vocabulary into their previous dialogue, and are acquiring some of the vocabulary needed for the ID card.

## 1(iii) Classroom objects

- This is the first set of nouns to be presented. Look carefully at the introduction to the pack for suggestions of use of flashcards, worksheets and games.
- For this first wordsearch, make it simple with illustrations so that pupils learn what to do; it may be useful here to let them have a first go at making one of their own. Do **not** worry if this does not work this first time – it is practice for later.
- Encourage active participation by getting pupils to not only point to, but get up and go to touch things.
- Say you want something (*Je voudrais*) with pupils coming to give the subject to you (*voilà*) again allowing movement around the class, which is vital for these pupils.
- True/false games – hold up objects/pictures saying *C'est un . . . .* Pupils have to decide *oui* or *non*; this can be the whole class calling out or teams or individuals.

### Assignment

- Classroom signs prepared by the pupils will give them confidence in their writing when they see them displayed for genuine information.
- The phrase book should be continued – this can either be done under topics or alphabetically.

## 1(iv) Getting involved

**Note:** teachers may use either form of the imperative. Sometimes the second person singular is preferred since pupils can easily respond with the *je* form which sounds the same.

●●●●●●●●●●●●●●●●●●●●●●●●●●●●●●●●●●●●●●●●●●

- The vocabulary in this topic relies heavily on mime and pupils can be encouraged to either mime as the teacher gives the order or give the order as the teacher mimes.
- Pupils can then guess what other pupils are miming.
- Flashcards of symbols will help with understanding, but pupils should be encouraged to think up their own symbols since they will be sure to understand these!
- Playing *Simon dit* will reinforce understanding and gives an opportunity for movement.

### Assignment

Pupils can now each make a classroom symbol with appropriate classroom language for display and daily reinforcement.

## 1(v) Numbers

- Present the numbers gradually throughout the whole module, 0–10, 11–20, 21–31.
- Do simple counting for sequence.
- Count objects in classroom.
- Do simple activities of missing numbers or what comes next?
- Introduce how to play Bingo and dominoes in class.

## Alphabet

The following thoughts on teaching the French alphabet may be of help.

Exactly half of the letters can be learned fairly effortlessly if pupils realize that:

- F L M N S Z sound virtually like their English equivalent.
- B C D G P T V rhyme in English, and so they do in French, though the sound of *'é'* will need practice.
- W follows on logically from V, particularly if written on board/O H P (as a double V), as it is said.
- J I X Y make you smile ( 'cheese' ). Y = *i grec*, should be explained.

- O Q U are pure sounds. Once the mouth-shape is formed, don't alter it!
- A and K rhyme.
- E 'hesitating' vowel. Sounds as if you can't remember. (Index finger to lower lip?)
- R: could do with some fresh R in here?

- This is introduced so that pupils can (a) spell important words like their name or town and (b) understand spellings so they can eventually correctly record things that have only been heard, e.g. on the telephone.
- The activities echo those suggested for numbers with sequencing, tunes/raps, missing letters, etc.
- The name cards could be used with letters blocked out for pupils to supply.

### Assignments

- Pupils can make up their own raps/songs using numbers and letters of the alphabet.
- Again pupil-produced display of numbers linked with numbers of objects reinforces concept of numbers as well as making classroom attractive.

## 1(vi) Personal details

- This now completes the basic information from 1(i) and 1(ii).
- Encourage pair/group work with simple interviews.
- Name, age, town cards can be given out for pupils to build up simulated personalities.

### Assignment

- Making up a dialogue and recording it is an opportunity to set up your system for pupils to record work. Not everyone will be able to do this successfully yet, but it is important practice for the rest of the course. It is usually enjoyed anyway.
- Using template 6 pupils can now make their own ID card which they could be encouraged to use in some real school situations, e.g. dinner pass, etc.

# MODULE 2 Talking about people

### Timescale
1 term

### Areas of experience
A    B

### Programme of study (part 1): Examples
Communicating in the target language
– ask for and give information
– express personal feelings and opinions

| Topics | Communicative objectives |
|---|---|
| (i)   Family members | Understanding and naming members of the family |
| (ii)  Family descriptions | Exchanging information about members of the family |
| (iii) Classmates | Reporting basic personal details about members of the class |
| (iv)  Pets | Understanding and naming pets |
| (v)   Likes and dislikes | Expressing personal opinions |

### Cross-curricular opportunities

| | |
|---|---|
| Designing and making (see assignments) | Design and Technology |
| Surveys | |
| Expressing opinions | PSE |

### Opportunities for assessment

| | |
|---|---|
| Respond to flashcards | AT1:1; AT2:1 |
| Understand names of family members | AT1:1 |
| Understand information given to others about family | AT1:1, 2, 3 |
| Ask/answer questions about people in family | AT1:2; AT2:1, 2 |
| Say one or two sentences about people in family | AT2:2, 3 |
| Draw a person from written description | AT3:1,2,3 |
| Complete written description from picture clues | AT4:1, 2, 3 |

### Assignments
Design and make a 'wanted' poster

Scrapbook/video on family/class

Talking photo album

Likes/dislikes survey

# Module 2 Talking about people          Topic (i) Family members

### Topic
(i) Family members

### Communicative objective
Understanding and naming members of the family

### Linguistic objectives (examples)
*ma famille*

*ma mère*

*mon père*

*ma sœur*

*mon frère*

*ma grand-mère*

*mon grand-père*

*Comment s'appelle ton . . . ?*
*ta . . . ?*

*Ma mère s'appelle . . .*

*Elle s'appelle . . .*

*Mon père s'appelle . . .*

*Il s'appelle . . .*

### Activities
- Linking family titles with flashcards and other pictures
- Naming members of picture families
- Worksheets for family
- Talking about own family
- Wordsearch
- Exchanging information about each other's families

### Resources
- Worksheets Set 1, 1–4
- Family flashcards
- Wordsearch, template 4a or 4b
- Blank wordsearch, template 4a
- Cue cards
- Name cards

- Pupils' family photos where possible
- Cut-outs of families from magazines, or individuals to make up families

### Assignments
Labelled photograph or drawing of own family

*LE FRANÇAIS, C'EST FACILE!*

# Module 2 Talking about people

# Topic (ii) Family descriptions

## Topic
(ii) Family descriptions

## Communicative objective
Exchanging information about members of the family

## Linguistic objectives (examples)

*Comment est ton/ta . . . ?*

*Il/Elle est grand(e)*
        *petit(e)*
        *gros(se)*
        *mince*

*Quel âge a ton frère?*
        *ta sœur?*

*Il/Elle a . . . ans*

## Activities
- Revision of numbers
- Talking about age of brothers/sisters
- Describing people from pictures/photos
- Worksheets linking descriptions with people
- Describing own family members
- Exchanging information about families
- Repetition 'chain'
- Song

## Resources
- Worksheets Set 2, 1 and 2
- Description flashcards
- Cue cards
- Number cards

- Magazine pictures/cartoons of different-sized people
- Song cassette

## Assignments
Scrapbook on family or talking photo album

# Module 2 Talking about people

# Topic (iii) Classmates

## Topic
(iii) Classmates

## Communicative objective
Reporting basic personal details about members of the class

## Linguistic objectives (examples)

*Comment s'appelle . . . ton ami(e)?*
*ton voisin?*
*ta voisine?*

*Il/Elle s'appelle . . .*

*Il/Elle a quel âge?*

*Il/Elle a . . . ans*

*Comment est . . . ?*

*Il/Elle est grand, etc.*

*Il/Elle a les cheveux blonds*
*marron*
*noirs*
*courts*
*frisés*
*longs*
*les yeux bleus*
*verts*
*bruns*

Note: *marron* **is an invariable adjective**

## Activities
- Build on 2(ii) for initial descriptions
- Worksheets about descriptions
- Drawing and colouring from information given (spoken or written)
- Completing a spoken or written description from visual clues
- Describing people in the class
- Guessing game from teacher's then pupils' descriptions
- Pairwork – information gap

## Resources
- Worksheets Set 2, 1 and 2
- Worksheet Set 3, 3 for listening (see Teaching notes page 109)
- Description flashcards
- Made-up wordsearch, template 4a or 4b
- Blank wordsearch, template 4a
- Picture/name/age (number) cards for sentence building

- Colour cards
- Pictures of heads showing different hair styles/colours

## Assignments
'Wanted' poster of real or imaginary person

# Module 2 Talking about people

# Topic (iv) Pets

## Topic
(iv) Pets

## Communicative objective
Understanding and naming pets

## Linguistic objectives (examples)

*Tu as un animal?*

*J'ai un chat*
   *un cheval*
   *un chien*
   *un cochon d'Inde*
   *un hamster*
   *un lapin*
   *un poisson rouge*
   *un serpent*
   *une souris*
   *une tortue*

## Activities
- Flashcard guessing games
- All games as suggested
- Worksheets Set 1, 1–4, Set 3, 1–2
- Wordsearch and making a wordsearch
- Drawing and labelling
- Questions and answers
- Song

## Resources
- Worksheets Set 1, 1–4, Set 3, 1–2
- Animal flashcards
- Pelmanism/snap cards, template 1
- Beetle, template 1
- Dominoes, template 2
- Bingo, template B2
- Made-up wordsearch, template 4a or 4b
- Blank wordsearch, template 4a
- Survey sheet, template 10

- Song cassette

## Assignments
Class display of labelled pictures (drawn or cut out) of pets

# Module 2 Talking about people

# Topic (v) Likes and dislikes

## Topic
(v) Likes and dislikes

## Communicative objective
Expressing personal opinions

## Linguistic objectives (examples)
*Tu aimes les chiens?*

*Oui*

*Non*

*J'aime . . .*

*Je n'aime pas . . .*

*J'adore . . .*

*Je déteste . . .*

*Je préfère . . .*

## Activities
- Linking likes and dislikes to pets
- Worksheets Set 2, 1–3
- Pelmanism and snap with likes/dislikes
- Record pupil preferences of animals on likes/dislikes sheets (Set 2, 4)
- Listening exercise
- Song

## Resources
- Worksheets Set 1 (any)
- Animal flashcards
- Likes/dislikes flashcards
- Worksheets Set 2, 1–4
- Likes/dislikes profile, template 9
- Survey sheet, template 10

- Song cassette

## Assignments
Class survey of likes/dislikes and pets

# Module 2: Talking about People

## 2(i) Family members

**Note:** although possessive pronouns and adjectival agreement come into this topic, there is no need, at this stage, for either to be taken as a teaching point. As only some pupils will manage such grammatical details, remember that effective communication is the aim.

- The best initial presentation for family members would be the teacher's own family with photographs.
- The flashcard family should be presented as just **a** family so that it can be linked by pupils with *mon/ma*, etc.
- Pictures of families could have one of the children circled as the spokesperson for naming the family, (we do not want to introduce *son/sa*, etc. here).
- Worksheets Set 1, 1–4 and made-up wordsearch can reinforce words.
- From photographs or drawings pupils can introduce/answer questions about their own family.
- Pupils can then exchange information about families.

**Note:** if *il/elle* is a problem, the pupil can simply say *Ma mère s'appelle . . .*, etc.

### Assignment

Pupils may now label a photograph of their own family if one is available or draw their family – *Voici mon père*, etc.

## 2(ii) Family descriptions

- After revision of numbers 1–20, elicit information about the ages of brothers and sisters (not parents because numbers above 31 have not yet been covered).
- After introduction of descriptions link these with pictures from magazines or cartoons.
- Worksheets Set 2, 1 and 2 will then link family member with description. It is probably best to leave sheet 3 at present because it is a more complicated exercise and these are early days in the learning process.
- Repetition 'chain' – to add variety to repetition, have pictures or OHTs, to make simple description, e.g. *Ma mère est petite*, and change either the person or the description – *Ma mère est grande* or *Mon père est petit*. This can be speeded up with sections of the class taking it in turns to respond.
- Pupils will then describe their own family using photographs and drawings.
- Pairwork – exchanging information about family members.

### Assignment

Pupils can build up a family scrapbook with photographs or drawings of family members and family activities, etc. **or** they can record onto cassette a presentation of their family, to link with a photo or drawing.

## 2(iii) Classmates

**Note:** this topic builds on 2(ii) with added detail, which may then be used to describe the family in more detail, but this is at the discretion of the teacher (pupils need variety, so this could be seen as too much of the same).

- After the initial presentation of new words, worksheets Set 2, 1 and 2 can link names and any kind of descriptive detail to encourage spoken or written sentences.
- Use worksheet Set 3, 3 for a listening activity. Pupils tick who is being described or sequence descriptions.
- Playing cards of nouns, ages and other descriptive details can then be used as a stimulus for lengthier spoken or written descriptions.
- 'Colour cards' can be made simply by cutting up card of different colours and writing the colour names on them.
- Teachers can give descriptive information for pupils to draw or colour from.
- Pairwork – information gap: pupils each draw a person and give information to each other to complete a second drawing and then compare pictures.

### Assignment

Pupils can make up 'wanted' posters with a drawing and a description below. If real people are chosen, e.g. teachers/famous people, etc. the sheets can be put around the room and form the source of a guessing game, i.e. **names** are not included on the poster.

## 2(iv) Pets

- This topic lends itself well to most of the games, so it is an excellent opportunity to teach the games themselves as well as the linguistic objectives.
- Using playing cards of animals, question and answer activities can be set up, e.g. cards face down on the table, one pupil picks one up, the other has to guess what it is: *Tu as un hamster? Non. Tu as une souris? Oui.* Then the other pupil has a turn. This can be scored but does not have to be.

- The survey sheet, template 10, is suggested here as a trial run of how to do a survey ready for 2(v). This time it is suggested that pupils' names/animals are ticked to find out who (or how many) has what.

### Assignment
Pupils draw or cut out animals and label them for an animal frieze or 'garden' of animals on Bingo template B2.

## 2(v) Likes and dislikes

- The heart symbols can be presented, repeated and reinforced with basic worksheets.
- Then link likes/dislikes with animals using pictures (board or OHT) and do Worksheets Set 2, 1–2, also 3 if pupils are ready for gap-filling.
- Elicit information from pupils. Then encourage pupils to exchange information.
- Pelmanism can be played as a stimulus for sentence-building based on pictures.
- The personal profile likes/dislikes sheet, template 9, can be started – the idea is that, if they are enlarged to A3, pupils can gradually add more details as further topics are completed.
- Pupils can have to listen for either **who** likes what or **what** is liked or disliked. Worksheets Set 2, 4 and Set 3, 3 (see introduction to worksheets).

### Assignment
The suggested survey will plot animals against heart symbols to get numbers of pupils who like/dislike, etc. certain animals.

# MODULE 3 My school

### Timescale
1 term

### Areas of experience
A

### Topics / Communicative objectives

| Topics | Communicative objectives |
|---|---|
| (i) Subjects | Understanding and naming school subjects |
| (ii) Likes and dislikes | Exchanging opinions about school subjects |
| (iii) Days of the week | Expressing opinions about days at school |
| (iv) The timetable | Exchanging information about the daily timetable |
| (v) Rooms in school | Understanding and naming the main points in the school and giving directions |

### Programme of study (part 1): Examples
Communicating in the target language
– express personal feeling and opinions
– conduct surveys
Understanding and responding
– follow directions and instructions

### Cross-curricular opportunities

| | |
|---|---|
| Number practice | Mathematics |
| Graphs | |
| Display design | Technology |
| School lay-out plan | |

### Opportunities for assessment

| | |
|---|---|
| Respond to flashcards/play games | AT1:1; AT2:1 |
| Understand names of subjects or rooms | AT1:1 |
| Understand other people's opinions about subjects | AT1:2 |
| Ask/answer survey questions | AT1:2; AT2:1,2,3 |
| Understand a simple timetable | AT3:1 |
| Complete a wordsearch | AT3:1 |
| Label pictures about school | AT4:1 |
| Write own timetable | AT4:1,2 |
| Write a few sentences about school | AT4:3 |

### Assignments
Labels for rooms in school/school subjects

Class survey/graph

Make up own school timetable

School plan (show visitor round)

# Module 3 My School

# Topic (i) Subjects

## Topic
(i) Subjects

## Communicative objective
Understanding and naming school subjects

## Linguistic objectives (examples)

*l'anglais*

*l'art/le dessin*

*le drame/le théâtre*

*le français*

*la géographie*

*l'histoire*

*l'informatique*

*les maths*

*la musique*

*la religion*

*les sciences*

*le sport*

*la technologie*

*Que fais-tu au collège?*

*Je fais . . .*

- teachers should choose those subjects appropriate to their pupils

## Activities
- Flashcard presentation
- Matching word and symbol
- Matching/memory games
- Worksheets Set 1, 1–4
- Wordsearch and making a wordsearch
- Drawing and labelling for display
- Play bingo level 1, template B3

## Resources
- Worksheets Set 1, 1–4
- Subject flashcards
- Variety of games from dominoes, template 2 snap/Pelmanism, template 1
- Made-up wordsearch, template 4b
- Blank wordsearch, template 4a
- Bingo level 1, template B3
- Cue cards

## Assignments
Labelled pictures of school subjects for classroom display

*LE FRANÇAIS, C'EST FACILE!*

# Module 3 My school

# Topic (ii) Likes and dislikes

## Topic
(ii) Likes and dislikes

## Communicative objective
Exchanging opinions about school subjects

## Linguistic objectives (examples)
Likes and dislikes – see vocabulary Module 2 (iv)

*Tu aimes . . . ?*

*Qu'est-ce que tu aimes?*

*Qu'est-ce que tu préfères?*

*Pourquoi?*

*C'est amusant*
> *casse-pieds*
> *difficile*
> *facile*
> *moche*
> *super*

## Activities
- Flashcard presentation
- Question and answer – class
- Worksheets Set 2, 1–4
  - making sentences
  - listen and draw
  - gap-filling
- Writing about likes/dislikes from profile, template 9
- Class survey with oral/written follow-up
- Pairwork ⎫
- Groupwork ⎬ oral
- Song

## Resources
- Worksheets Set 2, 1–3
- Subject flashcards
- Likes/dislikes flashcards
- Snap cards for matching/making up sentences
- Survey sheet, template 10
- Likes/dislikes profile, template 9

- Song cassette

## Assignments
Class survey

# Module 3 My school

# Topic (iii) Days of the week

## Topic
(iii) Days of the week

## Communicative objective
Expressing opinions about days at school

## Linguistic objectives (examples)
Days of the week (see templates 13a and 13b)

*Quel jour préfères-tu?*

*Mardi – c'est le français*

## Activities
- Flashcard presentation
- Linked presentation days and subjects
- Matching games/activities
- Days of the week rap
- Pairwork – sequencing days
- Pairwork – making up words from syllables
- Copy-writing
- Questions and answers about opinions
- Building picture sentences
- Song

## Resources
- Subject flashcards
- Likes and dislikes flashcards
- Days of the week cue cards, templates 13a and 13b
- Cut-up day cards for re-arranging syllables. (See Teaching notes page 117.)
- Snap cards, template 1
- Made-up wordsearch, template 4a or 4b

- Song cassette

## Assignments
Working towards a timetable

# Module 3 My school

# Topic (iv) The timetable

**Topic**
(iv) The timetable

**Communicative objective**
Exchanging information about the daily timetable

**Linguistic objectives (examples)**

days of the week

numbers 1–10

opinions vocabulary

*l'emploi du temps*

*la leçon*

*le déjeuner*

*la récréation*

*le matin*

*l'après-midi*

*avant*

*après*

**Activities**

- OHP/board – large timetable to fill in
- Questions and answers
- Bingo with days and subjects
- Oral and written work, worksheets Set 2
- Daily timetable
- Battleships (days/subjects)

**Resources**

- Flashcards subjects
              timetable
- Worksheets Set 2
- Day cards
- Bingo timetable, templates B3 and B4
- Battleships, blank template 5b

**Assignments**
Make up own school timetable

# Module 3 My school

# Topic (v) Rooms in school

## Topic
(v) Rooms in school

## Communicative objective
Understanding and naming the main points in the school and giving directions

## Linguistic objectives (examples)
*la bibliothèque*

*le bureau*

*la cantine*

*le collège*

*le couloir*

*la cour*

*le gymnase*

*le laboratoire*

*la réception*

*la salle de classe*

*le terrain de sport*

*la salle de* + subjects

*C'est à droite*
    *à gauche*

*Tournez/Tourne*

*Allez/Va tout droit*

*Voici/Voilà*

## Activities
- Rooms in school flashcards, then combine with directions
- Snap and Pelmanism matching words and pictures
- Worksheets Set 1, 1–4
- Worksheet Set 2, 1–2 linking position and places in school
- Wordsearch and making a wordsearch
- Follow spoken directions referring to plan on OHP
- Follow directions in school corridors, etc.
- Song

## Resources
- Worksheets Set 1, 1–4
- Worksheets Set 2, 1–2
- School flashcards
- Pelmanism/snap, template 1
- Made-up wordsearch, template 4b
- Blank wordsearch, template 4a
- Cue cards

- Simple plan of school on OHP
- Song cassette

## Assignments
Making up a plan of the school

Showing someone around the school

*LE FRANÇAIS, C'EST FACILE!*

# Module 3: My school

## 3(i) Subjects

See introduction for all suggested activities.

**Assignment**

Pupils draw symbols for school subjects and label them for display.

## 3(ii) Likes and dislikes

- Link these flashcards with subjects to elicit: *J'aime ( le sport).*
- Two cards presented to individuals to elicit similar sentence.
- Pupil picks two cards, shows class subject only. Teacher: *Tu aimes . . . ?* Pupil answers according to cards in hand *Oui, j'aime* or *Non, je déteste . . . .*
- Using small-sized cards pupil makes up own picture sentences showing personal likes and dislikes. These can be the basis for oral or written work as well as pair/group question and answer work.

**Preference**

- Use **préférer** + subject flashcards.
  Question: *Tu préfères le . . . ou le . . . ?* Teacher removes one card and says. *Je préfère le . . .*
- Practise above, letting pupils remove one card, leaving the one they prefer in each case.
- Pupils can then be given two subject cards and answer questions referring to them, holding up their preference.

**Opinions**

- Presentation of pairs of flashcards to elicit *Le français, c'est amusant*, etc.
- Pupil fixes pairs of cards on board for class to describe.
- Similar work in pairs/groups with smaller cards, leading to oral or written work.

**Linking likes and dislikes to opinions**

- Use the three sets of flashcards to build up picture sentences for oral and/or written work, e.g. subject, preference, opinion.
- Smaller cards can be given out to pupils to make picture sentences describing their own opinions, e.g. *J'aime l'anglais, c'est amusant*, etc.

**Assignment**

- To do survey, use blank sheet – pupils plot names against subjects and put like/dislike symbol in the squares.
- Use the completed survey for oral work, e.g. *Qui aime le . . . ? Combien d'élèves détestent le . . . ?*

## 3(iii) Days of the week

- Present days of the week with word cue cards.
- Activities from the front for pupils to practise sequencing these.
- Sets of day cards to pairs/groups to do the same.
- These could then be carefully copied.
- Large cue cards cut up into halves/syllables for pupils to rebuild words – at front of class. Cut *lu/ndi* not *lun/di*, etc. or all combinations will be correct.
- Smaller sets of above for pair/group work.
- Wordsearch.

**Introducing timetable and opinions**

- Link days with subjects, just as lists under days at this stage.
- Pupils come out and build up their lists for different days.
- With days and subjects on OHP/board put like symbol next to a subject to present: *Quel jour préfères-tu? Lundi, c'est le français!*

**Assignment**

Pupils can be beginning to build up their timetable ready for Topic (iv).

## 3(iv) The timetable

- On a large blank timetable fill in days and lesson numbers e.g. 1–5 (time need not be introduced).
- At this stage vocabulary for break, lunch, morning, afternoon, before and after can be introduced at the teacher's discretion.
- Play bingo levels 2 and 3. Level 2 – lessons are put on particular days so the day and the lesson need to be as the teacher calls them out; Level 3 can be further complicated by lessons being inserted in particular slots on particular days.
- Play battleships, putting days against subjects on the grid.
- Give pupils individual blank timetables to fill in with pictures/words.
- Questions and answers about where lessons are on the timetable.

**Assignment**

On the blank timetable (bingo template B5) pupils can draw or write in their own or an ideal timetable. Teachers may need to supply their own blank if their school timetable differs from the one supplied.

## 3(v) Rooms in school

• See introduction for all suggested activities.

**Directions**

• Picture/cue cards around class for pupils to direct each other.
• Simple plan of school on board/OHP as stimulus for oral/written work.
• Worksheets Set 2 will link position/direction and room.

**Assignment**

If the school plan is complex, provide a clear outline for pupils. To show someone around, indicate rooms with *Voici* or *Voilà* + name of room.

# MODULE 4 Where we live

### Timescale
1 term

### Areas of experience
A    C

### Programme of study (part 1): Examples
Communicating in the target language

– take part in structured role play

– copy phrases and sentences

Understanding and responding

– follow directions and instructions

| Topics | Communicative objectives |
|---|---|
| (i) Homes | Exchanging information about types of home |
| (ii) Location | Exchanging information about where the home is |
| (iii) Rooms | Understanding and naming the rooms in the house |
| (iv) Directions | Understanding and saying where rooms are in the house |
| (v) Furniture | Understanding and naming articles of furniture |
| (vi) The house | Exchanging detailed information about the home |

### Cross-curricular opportunities

| | |
|---|---|
| Designing and making | Design and Technology |
| Understanding that different people have different homes | PSE |

### Opportunities for assessment

| | |
|---|---|
| Respond to flashcards | AT1:1; AT2:1 |
| Understand names of rooms/furniture | AT1:1 |
| Understand where rooms are in house | AT1:2,3 |
| Ask/answer questions about where people live | AT1:2; AT2:1,2 |
| Say/record a few sentences about ideal house | AT2:2,3 |
| Match room/furniture words with pictures | AT3:1 |
| Draw house/room from written description | AT3:1,2,3 |
| Label rooms in house | AT4:1 |
| Write a few sentences about ideal house | AT4:3 |

### Assignments
Scrapbook

Design a house

Design and make estate agent's poster/circular

Interview other people about their home (audio or video)

# Module 4 Where we live

# Topic (i) Homes

## Topic
(i) Homes

## Communicative objective
Exchanging information about types of home

## Linguistic objectives (examples)
*un appartement*

*un garage*

*un jardin*

*une maison*

*C'est grand*
> *petit*

*Où habites-tu?*

*J'habite une maison*

*Où habite Pierre?*

*Il habite un appartement*

*Il y a . . .(?)*

*Oui*

*Non*

## Activities
- Flashcard presentation
- Questions and answers about selves
- Questions about others (class and flashcard)
- Pairwork – simulation
- Drawing and labelling
- Collage and captions
- Song

## Resources
- House flashcards
- Cue cards
- French name cue cards, template 15

- Magazines for cutting up
- Realia from France; you can **send** for:
  - leaflets showing houses from *notaire*
  - newspapers for adverts
  - pictures of French houses
- Song cassette

## Assignments
Working towards collage and caption display work (Topic ii)

# Module 4 Where we live

# Topic (ii) Location

### Topic
(ii) Location

### Communicative objective
Exchanging information about where the home is

### Linguistic objectives (examples)
*Où habites-tu?*

*(À Plymouth) en Angleterre*

*Où habite Annick?*

*(À Morlaix) en France*

*Tu habites dans une ville?*
        *un village?*
        *à la campagne?*
        *au bord de la mer?*

### Activities
- Flashcard/cue card presentation
- Pairwork – role play/information gap
- Matching word/picture
- Worksheets Set 2, 1–3. Use two details in each case from people/town/country/type of dwelling/area
- Making sentences
- Matching/making speech bubbles with stimulus pictures

### Resources
- Worksheets Set 2, 1–3
- Flashcards – as linguistic objectives
- Made-up wordsearch, template 4b, with French towns, template 17
- Blank speech bubbles, template 7
- Town cue cards

- Sentence cards cut up for re-making
- Magazines and realia (copies) to cut up

### Assignments
Collage of people, homes, location and country with speech bubbles to make illustration = creative work for display

# Module 4 Where we live

# Topic (iii) Rooms

### Topic
(iii) Rooms

### Communicative objective
Understanding and naming the rooms in the house

### Linguistic objectives (examples)
une chambre

une cuisine

un escalier

une pièce

une salle de bains

une salle à manger

un salon

une toilette

numbers 1–10

Décris ta maison

Il y a

C'est une maison avec

À vendre

### Activities
- Flashcard presentation
- Worksheets matching words/pictures
- Pupils build up house on OHT
- Questions and answers about own house
- Pairwork – getting information/information gap simulation
- Speaking/writing about own home
- IT opportunity

### Resources
- Worksheets Set 1, 1–4
- Rooms flashcards
- Bingo, template B6
- Beetle, template 1 (sets of rooms)
- Made-up wordsearch
- OHT house and furniture
- Cue cards

- French magazines for illustrations

### Assignments
Design an ideal house/flat

Estate agent's poster of house for sale

# Module 4 Where we live

# Topic (iv) Directions

## Topic
(iv) Directions

## Communicative objective
Understanding and saying where rooms are in the house

## Linguistic objectives (examples)
*Où est . . . ?*

*au rez-de-chaussée*

*au premier étage*

*à droite*

*à gauche*

*à côté de*

*en face de*

*entre*

## Activities
- Flashcard presentation of 'position' words
- Practice:
  – using true/false
  – teacher describes, pupils come out and match pictures (OHP or board)
- Pupils complete plan from instructions (spoken/written)
- Worksheets Set 2, 1–2
- Song cassette

## Resources
- Flashcards showing pairs of rooms
- Worksheets Set 2, 1–2
- Bingo, template B6
- Prepared commentary (teacher) of position of rooms in houses for listening practice
- Sentence cards for matching with pictures

- Song cassette

## Assignments
Recorded commentary to show a visitor around the already designed ideal home

# Module 4 Where we live

# Topic (v) Furniture

## Topic
(v) Furniture

## Communicative objective
Understanding and naming articles of furniture

## Linguistic objectives (examples)
*une armoire*

*un canapé*

*une chaîne* or *un hi-fi*

*une chaise*

*un fauteuil*

*un lit*

*un placard*

*des rideaux*

*une table*

*un tapis*

*une télévision*

## Activities
- Flashcard presentation
- Worksheets for recognition
- Matching games
- Bingo levels 1–3
- Wordsearch
- Building up rooms – OHT/pictures/cut-outs
- Noughts and crosses

## Resources
- Worksheets Set 1, 1–4, Set 3, 1–2
- Furniture flashcards
- Snap/Pelmanism, template 1
- Beetle, template 1
- Bingo, template B6
- Made-up wordsearch, template 4a or 4b
- Noughts and crosses, template 3a and 3b
- OHT pictures of rooms
- Furniture cue cards

- Magazines for cutting up

## Assignments
Design a room, draw it or make a collage, labelled

*LE FRANÇAIS, C'EST FACILE!*

# Module 4 Where we live

# Topic (vi) The house

● ● ● ● ● ● ● ● ● ● ● ● ● ● ● ● ● ● ● ● ● ● ● ● ● ● ● ● ● ● ● ● ●

## Topic
(vi) The house

## Communicative objective
Exchanging detailed information about the home

## Linguistic objectives (examples)
*Dans la/ta maison il y a . . . ?*

*Oui*

*Non*

*Qu'est-ce qu'il y a dans la/ta maison?*

*Il y a . . .*

rooms

furniture

colours from 2(iii)

*blanc*

*rouge*

*jaune*

*noir*

## Activities
- Matching furniture to rooms:
  – flashcards
  – OHTs
  – Worksheets Set 2 using the double-box to link furniture with room
- Teacher-led then pairwork questions and answers about ideal room (previous assignment) or rooms of own home
- Song

## Resources
- Worksheets Set 2, 1–3
- All module 4 flashcards
- Bingo, template B6
- Beetle, template 1, rooms or furniture
- All module 4 cue cards

---

- Magazine pictures of rooms
- Song cassette

## Assignments
Recorded or written description of own room/any room of own home (illustrated) or of ideal room (previous assignment)

● ● ● ● ● ● ● ● ● ● ● ● ● ● ● ● ● ● ● ● ● ● ● ● ● ● ● ● ● ● ● ● ●

# Module 4: Where we live

## General notes on the module

### Resources

Pictures of old and modern French houses would be useful – possible sources:
- French magazines
- Photographs
- House sale adverts from newspapers or from *Notaire/Immobilier* offices

Also, plenty of English magazines with pictures of rooms and furniture for assignments and general illustration. In fact, all illustrations for this module can either be cut out from magazines, or made from the visuals supplied, or drawn.

### Games

Bingo level 1 – furniture, one item in any room AT1: 1
2 – furniture in a particular room AT1: 2
3 – more than one item in each room
Beetle – collect either rooms to complete house, or furniture to complete room(s).

### 4(i) Homes

- The initial flashcard presentation of the new vocabulary is no real problem because the vocabulary is so limited in this topic.
- The use of *Il/Elle habite* as well as *J'habite* will need a lot of practice in a variety of ways.
- For this, names of pupils can be used, or French name cards given out, or name cards linked with cut-out people from magazines.
- Spoken/written accounts can be built up using pictures of people, name cue cards, home vocabulary, e.g. *Paul habite une maison, c'est grande. Il y a un jardin.*
- Groups/pairs of pupils could build up the picture sentence and then either match it to phrase cards or write their own sentences (practice for the assignment).

**Assignment**
Pupils can start to write sentences to match pictures ready for 4(ii).

### 4(ii) Location

- This topic builds on (i), adding more information, including towns, country and locations.
- As in 4(i) picture sentences can be made, this time including town name, country and exact location.
- The worksheets allow a variety of linked information to build sentences, or to use for gap-filling (Set 2, sheet 3).
- The pairwork can be a simulation or a gap-filling exercise, with pupils given complete or incomplete information about imaginary people to exchange.
- Speech bubbles could then be matched to illustrations of such information.
- And finally, speech bubbles could be written by pupils for the above.

**Assignment**
The pupils now build up their own collage with appropriate speech bubbles. This could be individual, pair or group work.

### 4(iii) Rooms

- Present new vocabulary by using flashcards and Worksheets Set 1, 1–4
- Using the board and flashcards or OHP, pupils can follow instructions: *Mettez la cuisine dans la maison*, etc.
- Pupils can then list the rooms seen in the house. *Dans la maison il y a . . .*
- At this stage numbers can also be added. Beetle could now be played to build up a house.
- Question and answer work about rooms in their own homes is now appropriate, followed by pairwork, e.g. information gap or interviewing one another.

**Assignment**
The assignment simply allows creative use of the newly-acquired vocabulary, encouraging labelling and simple description (remember all written work can be alternatively spoken and recorded).

### 4(iv) Directions

- A simple outline for 'upstairs/downstairs' will initially place rooms.
- Using pairs of pictures, *à droite/à gauche* can be introduced.
- Using three or more pictures *à côté, entre* or *de* can be presented.
- *En face de* will be more easily explained using the house plan.
- Do plenty of work with pupils and where they sit in class to present these positions.
- Worksheets Set 2, 1 and 2 can then combine a room and its position.
- A lot of activities where pupils match pictures to information will be needed here.

**Assignment**
This could be recorded or written as appropriate.

## 4(v) Furniture

- Do the flashcard presentation and Worksheets Set 1 using only five or six items at a time.
- Most of the games can be used, but in particular bingo (all levels) and beetle.
- Rooms can be built up in the same way as the house was in (iii).
- If teachers wish they can add furniture/appliances for the bathroom and kitchen but it was felt that, for most pupils, the topic already had sufficient content.

### Assignment

This could be used as a cross-curricular activity with technology.

## 4(vi) The house

- This topic allows all of the information from the rest of the module to be drawn together in a fairly detailed project.
- Write the colour names on coloured card for flashcards.
- All previous activities can be re-used, encouraging pupils to give as much information as possible about their house including rooms and furniture.
- Worksheets Set 2, 1–3 can be used for writing or reading (give either pictures or words) using rooms and items of furniture, and for gap-filling if sheet 3 is included.
- The higher levels of bingo here are also appropriate.
- Pupils should be encouraged to talk about their last assignment, an ideal room.
- Discussion can then be done on their own homes and rooms and, in particular, their own bedroom.

### Assignment

This has been left open in order to encourage pupils to choose their own topic, to round off the module; this can be presented in either a written or spoken form.

# MODULE 5 A Visit to France

## Timescale
1 term

## Areas of experience
A   B   C   E

## Topics / Communicative objectives

| Topics | Communicative objectives |
|---|---|
| (i) Getting there | Understanding and naming means of getting to France |
| (ii) Shops | Understanding and naming types of shop in France |
| (iii) Food | Understanding and asking for food items |
| (iv) Money | Operating with French money |
| (v) Buying food | Asking for food for a picnic or snack |

## Programme of study (part 1): Examples
Communicating in the target language

– take part in structured role play

Developing cultural awareness

– learn the use of social conventions

Understanding and responding

– listen for detail

## Cross-curricular opportunities

| | |
|---|---|
| Designing and making | Design and Technology |
| Shopping and money | Maths |
| Planning and sharing | PSE |

## Opportunities for assessment

| | |
|---|---|
| Respond to flashcards | AT1:1; AT2:1,2 |
| Understand names of shops/put in order heard | AT1:1 |
| Play games using shop/food names | AT1:1,2; AT2:1,2 |
| Take part in shop dialogue | AT1:1,2; AT2:1,2,3 |
| Complete shop wordsearch | AT3:1 |
| Put written dialogue in correct order | AT3:2,3 |
| Label transport/shop pictures | AT4:1 |
| Write/complete shop dialogue | AT4:1,2,3 |

## Assignments
Map with ferry routes marked

Design and make labels for shops

Display of labelled foods

Set up classroom shop/café

Shopkeeper/customer scene

# Module 5 A visit to France

# Topic (i) Getting there

## Topic
(i) Getting there

## Communicative objective
Understanding and naming means of getting to France

## Linguistic objectives (examples)
*Voici*

*l'Angleterre*

*la France*

*la Manche*

*Londres*

*Paris*

*On traverse la Manche*

*On prend l'aéroglisseur*
> *l'avion*
> *le bateau/le ferry*
> *le train*
> *le tunnel*
> *la voiture*

## Activities
- Flashcard presentation
- Mimes and sound effects for means of travel
- Recognizing means of travel from brochures and categorizing
- Drawing/labelling transport
- Worksheets Set 1, 1–4
- Wordsearch
- OHT putting on ferry routes/air route
- Song

## Resources
- Worksheets Set 1, 1–4
- Transport flashcards
- Map of routes, template 11
- Snap/Pelmanism, template 1
- Made-up wordsearch, template 4b
- Transport cue cards
- OHT map with routes as overlays, template 11

- Brochures from cross-channel ferries for pictures of ferries/hovercraft, etc. or magazine pictures
- Song cassette

## Assignments
Enlarged map with ferry and air (London–Paris) routes marked and illustrated with pictures of means of travel and other items linked with travel, e.g. cases, bags, etc.

# Module 5 A visit to France

# Topic (ii) Shops

**Topic**
(ii) Shops

**Communicative objective**
Understanding and naming types of shop in France

**Linguistic objectives (examples)**
*la boucherie*

*la boulangerie*

*la charcuterie*

*l'épicerie/l'alimentation*

*l'hypermarché*

*le magasin*

*le marché*

*le supermarché*

*le tabac*

**Activities**
- Flashcard guessing games
- Matching activities/games
- Worksheets Set 1, 1–4
- Missing letter shop signs
- Jumbled syllable shop signs
- Wordsearch
- Categorizing food, etc. (**not** named at this stage) into correct shop

**Resources**
- Worksheets Set 1, 1–4
- Shop flashcards
- Food flashcards
- Shop name cards
- Snap/Pelmanism, template 1
- Made-up wordsearch, template 4b
- Blank wordsearch, template 4b
- Shop pictures with letters missing from labels
- Cut-up shop name cards, template 12a-c

- Magazine pictures of food or packets/labels, etc.

**Assignments**
Classroom display with shop names above large window (card) for pupils
to stick on cut-outs/ drawings, categorizing types of food sold in each shop

# Module 5 A visit to France

# Topic (iii) Food

### Topic
(iii) Food

### Communicative objective
Understanding and asking for food items

### Linguistic objectives (examples)
la baguette

le croissant

les bonbons

les chips

le chocolat

les frites

le fromage

la glace

le jambon

le saucisson

la bière

le café

le coca

la limonade

le thé

le vin

la banane

l'orange

la pomme

le raisin

la tomate

Je voudrais . . . s'il vous plaît (s.v.p.)

Merci

### Activities
- Flashcard guessing games
- Matching activities words/pictures
- Worksheets Set 1, 1–4, Set 3, 1–2 to reinforce vocabulary
- Worksheets Set 2, 1–3, linking food with appropriate shops
- Kim's game
- Pelmanism
- Food bingo
- Sequencing of food asked for, Worksheet Set 3, 3
- Categorizing items into shops (window display)
- Labelling food
- Putting pictures in alphabetical order
- Song

### Resources
- Worksheets Set 1, 1–4, Set 2, 1–3, Set 3, 1–3
- Food flashcards
- Snap/Pelmanism, template 1
- Dominoes, template 2
- Made-up wordsearch, template 4a or 4b
- Bingo template B7
- Cue cards

- Made-up shopping lists of words with letters missing or pictures
- Tray and objects
- Where possible:
  – empty containers of French food
  – French magazine pictures of food
  – plastic food
- Song cassette

### Assignments
Display of labelled food, completing the previous assignment of making up shop windows

*LE FRANÇAIS, C'EST FACILE!*

# Module 5 A visit to France

# Topic (iv) Money

## Topic
(iv) Money

## Communicative objective
Operating with French money

## Linguistic objectives (examples)
*l'argent français*

*un billet de (100) francs*

*un centime*

*un franc*

*une pièce de (20) centimes*

*C'est combien?*

Numbers – as appropriate

e.g. 30, 40, 50, 60 (70, 80, 90), 100

**Note:**

9,50F
9F50 } = *neuf francs cinquante*

## Activities
- Familiarization with French money
- Counting – higher numbers
- Counting out coins and notes
- Pelmanism using word and price cards
- Listening for prices, Worksheet Set 3, 3
- Worksheets Set 2, 1–2, linking prices with food
- Simple scenes
- Deciding how much money to hand over
- Song

## Resources
- Worksheets Set 2, 1–2
- Worksheets Set 3, 3, filled in with food and prices
- Pelmanism, template 1
- Number cards

- Made-up price tags
- Real, plastic or photocopied currency
- Song cassette

## Assignments
Working towards the classroom shop or café, and shopkeeper or waiter and customer scene

# Module 5 A visit to France

# Topic (v) Buying food

## Topic
(v) Buying food

## Communicative objective
Asking for food for a picnic or snack

## Linguistic objectives (examples)
greetings

*Vous désirez?*

*Je voudrais . . . s'il vous plaît*

*une bouteille de . . .*

*un (demi) kilo de . . .*

*un paquet de . . .*

*un sandwich au fromage*
*          au jambon*

*un croque-monsieur*

drinks for café scene – see 5(iii)

*C'est tout?*

*C'est combien?*

*Voilà*

*monsieur*

*madame*

## Activities
- Revise greetings
- Demonstrate asking for required amounts of food
- Matching containers and foods, i.e. appropriateness
- Worksheets Set 2, 1–3, linking amounts/containers with food and drink
- Worksheets Set 2, 5a and 5b, dialogue – build up dialogue
- Bingo – snacks
- Pairwork and groupwork
- Building up dialogues for café or shop
- Song

## Resources
- Food and drink flashcards
- Bingo, template B8
- Worksheets Set 2, 1–3, 5a and 5b

---

- As many props as possible for shop/café scene:
  – empty French food packets
  – empty English packets relabelled (by pupils?)
  – plastic food
- Magazine pictures
- Price tags
- Bags for shopping
- Shopping lists
- Plastic cups for café
- Song cassette

## Assignments
Set up classroom shop/café

Make up scene with customer and shopkeeper or waiter

Possibly set up a real snack bar one breaktime with croissants (if available), sweets, crisps, fruit and drinks

# Module 5: A visit to France

## 5(i) Getting there

- You need to do work with maps of all kinds to ensure understanding of the relative positions of France and England, and to do lots of matching/repetition to get across the French names of the countries, the Channel, London, etc.
- You do not need to use all of the routes available – possibly choose to focus on the ones most relevant to your position.
- If the map is copied onto an OHT the routes can be overlaid as well as, eventually, OHT cut-outs of the means of transport appropriately placed.
- Remember to put the tunnel route in now!
- For presentation of the transport vocabulary use all the guessing and matching activities and games.
- Get the pupils to think up mimes and sound-effects for each one to give variety to recognition activities.
- Cross-Channel travel brochures with pictures and details of routes to France will be good general experience for pupils.

**Note:** the use of *on* here facilitates in a simple way talking about travel to France in general, but *je* could be used if teachers prefer. However *on* is useful for any general comments later, e.g. what shops sell, etc.

### Assignment
Using drawings and cut-outs pupils can make a large display about travel to and from France.

## 5(ii) Shops

- At this point in the visit, the shops are merely being named, not used, so, although some activities suggest recognition through categorizing goods for sale, these need not be named in French yet.
- With the large shop name cards (enlarged) you can begin to build up a display of a row of shops on the classroom wall, with a large card beneath each one as the shop window, where pictures can be affixed and labelled (iii).
- Copy the shop signs and blank out some letters to give practice in spelling them – also 'which letter is missing?' gives alphabet practice.
- With the wordsearch, do not overlook the possibility of pupils designing their own for use in class.

### Assignment
Building up the large shop wall display (see above).

## 5(iii) Food

**Note:** teachers are advised to use the food items which they feel are most appropriate to the group of pupils. These have been presented in three groups: (a) groceries/snacks, (b) drinks, (c) fruit and vegetables.

- This is a good module for pupils to get the opportunity to handle things – empty packets or plastic bottles, etc. You can always relabel British items in French.
- Do not present too many new words at once and do not over-use the basic worksheets – other activities such as picture/word shopping lists would practise the same reading, understanding, writing skills and give variety, which is vital.
- Kim's game is a good one here, particularly if one category of foods is used at a time.
- Putting pictures in alphabetical order is an introduction to dictionary skills – do not give more than five or six at a time and encourage a little rap or tune to be made up when the list is correct.
- Although not suggested as a core activity, pupils could revise likes/dislikes here using either the personal *j'aime/je n'aime pas* sheets, template 9, or the listening worksheet, Set 2, sheet 4.
- The boundary between the shop and café has been left deliberately vague here since pupils are simply practising asking for what they want, no matter what the situation.

### Assignment
The display of labelled foods could be empty English packets relabelled in French, or labelled pictures (drawn or cut out).

## 5(iv) Money

**Note:** the amount of detail done in this module will depend on the teacher's knowledge of the pupils involved.

- The central point is that they should have a basic understanding of French currency.
- They also need to know how much money they would need to give to cover the cost of an item requested, e.g. if the item is 3.50F they would give 4F and receive change, i.e. teach them to 'round up'.
- Some teachers might consider it helpful to their understanding of approximate values of coins, etc. to compare them with the English, i.e. shape, size, colour, etc. Depending upon the pupils' ability teachers may want to give a very approximate idea of the exchange rate here or in module 9 so that prices will be realistic.
- Make up price tags to get pupils used to saying French amounts.
- Pairwork can come from using Pelmanism – picture cards and price tags so that as each pupil

**Teaching notes 5**

turns a card over the one with food asks: *C'est combien une glace?* and the other with the price card says: *C'est 4 francs*, etc.
- Because of the importance for pupils going to France to understand prices over the counter, i.e. spoken, plenty of listening activities need to be done with prices, probably with pupils initially ticking the correct one of four, and eventually writing the prices they hear in figures.

**Assignment**
Simple dialogues and making/labelling packets, etc. in preparation for the next assignment.

## 5(v) Buying Food
- Revise greetings for the eventual role play.
- Learning the vocabulary for containers, amounts and numbers for shopping is important because pupils also learn what is appropriate.
- More vocabulary for a picnic or snack can be taken from the full food list if required.

- Using picture cards (snap size) get pupils to match containers/weights and foods.
- The double worksheets, Set 2, can then be used to practise this.
- It would be nice to record pairs or groups on cassette and even on video.

**Dialogue pattern (guidance only):**
- *Bonjour monsieur.*
- *Bonjour madame.*
- *Vous désirez?*
- *Une bouteille de limonade s.v.p.*
- *Voilà. C'est tout?*
- *Une glace s.v.p.*
- *C'est tout?*
- *Oui. C'est combien?*
- *6F madame.*
- *Voilà.*
- *Merci. Au revoir.*
- *Au revoir.*

# MODULE 6 At home

● ● ● ● ● ● ● ● ● ● ● ● ● ● ● ● ● ● ● ● ● ● ● ● ● ● ● ● ● ● ● ● ● ● ● ● ● ● ● ● ● ● ●

## Timescale
1 term

## Areas of experience
A   B   D

## Topics / Communicative objectives

| Topics | Communicative objectives |
|---|---|
| (i) Family hobbies | Exchanging information about how family members spend their time |
| (ii) Meals | Exchanging information about meals |
| (iii) Who does what? | Exchanging information about the division of household tasks |
| (iv) At the table | Coping at mealtimes |

## Assignments
Survey of home hobbies/graph

Role play at meal table

Family album with cassette

## Programme of study (part 1): Examples
Communicating in the target language

– find out and give information

– copy phrases and sentences

Developing language-learning skills

– learn short texts (song)

Developing the ability to work with others

– take part in language games

## Cross-curricular opportunities

| | |
|---|---|
| Graphs | Maths |
| Family life | } PSE |
| Different types of families | |

## Opportunities for assessment

| | |
|---|---|
| Respond to flashcards | AT1:1; AT2:1,2 |
| Understand hobbies/tasks | AT1:1,2 |
| Ask/answer questions about what other people do | AT1:1,2; AT2:1,2 |
| Say a few sentences about what people do | AT2:2,3 |
| Match words to pictures | AT3:2 |
| Build sentences using cut-up sentence cards | AT3:2,3 |
| Copy sentences about tasks/hobbies | AT4:2 |
| Write simple sentences about tasks/hobbies | AT4:3 |

● ● ● ● ● ● ● ● ● ● ● ● ● ● ● ● ● ● ● ● ● ● ● ● ● ● ● ● ● ● ● ● ● ● ● ● ● ● ● ● ● ● ●

# Module 6 At home

# Topic (i) Family hobbies

## Topic
(i) Family hobbies

## Communicative objective
Exchanging information on how family members spend their time

## Linguistic objectives (examples)

| Que | fais-tu | | |
| | fait | ta mère | à la maison? |
| | | ton père | |
| | | ta sœur | |
| | | ton frère | |
| Je/Il/Elle | bricole | | |
| | écoute | les cassettes | |
| | | les disques | |
| | | la musique | |
| | | la radio | |
| | joue | à l'ordinateur | |
| | | aux cartes | |
| | | avec des amis | |
| | parle | avec des amis | |
| | regarde | la télé | |
| | | le journal | |
| | | un magazine | |

## Activities
- Revise members of family from 2(i)
- Presentation of hobbies
- Mime and say
- Match words and pictures
- Talking about what other people do
- Worksheets Set 1 and Set 2, linking family members with hobbies
- Wordsearch
- Pairwork – gap-filling, using Worksheet Set 2, 3
- Copy-writing
- Sentence-building
- Writing simple sentences
- Song

## Resources
- Worksheets Set 1, 1–4, Set 2, 1–3
- Flashcards – the house
    - family
    - hobbies
    - some target language verbs from topic 1(iv)
- Speech bubbles, template 7
- Made-up wordsearch, template 4b
- Pelmanism, template 1
- Cue cards

- Magazine pictures or advertisements of activities
- Cut-up sentence cards
- Family name cards
- Song cassette

## Assignments
Picture and caption display to show pupils' family interests

Survey of family hobbies

# Module 6 At home

# Topic (ii) Meals

## Topic
(ii) Meals

## Communicative objective
Exchanging information about meals

## Linguistic objectives (examples)

*le petit déjeuner*

*le déjeuner*

*le goûter*

*le dîner*

- see teaching notes

*C'est à huit heures*
    *une heure*
    *quatre heures*
    *six heures*

*Tu prends . . . ?*

*C'est quel repas?*

*Où mange ta famille?*

*dans la cuisine*

*dans la salle à manger*

*devant la télé*

*Qu'est-ce que tu manges pour . . . ?*

- make a choice from the general food list, including something appropriate for each meal. The amount of vocabulary included here is at the teacher's discretion.

## Activities
- Presentation of meals with appropriate times
- Linking meals with food – reading, speaking, writing
- Linking meals with appropriate rooms
- Worksheets Set 1
- Worksheets Set 2
- Wordsearch
- Sentence-building orally and written from pictures/words
- Kim's game
- Beetle
- Song

## Resources
- Worksheets Set 1, 1–4
- Worksheets Set 2, 1–3
- Flashcards – food
  - meals
  - four mealtimes
  - rooms
- Beetle – sets of food to make meals
- Made-up wordsearch, template 4b
- Snap picture/word cards, template 1
- Cue cards

- Magazine pictures for collage
- Appropriate empty packets, etc.
- Song cassette

## Assignments
Labelled collage or drawings of typical meals for display

# Module 6 At home

# Topic (iii) Who does what?

## Topic

(iii) Who does what?

## Communicative objective

Exchanging information about the division of household tasks

## Linguistic objectives (examples)

*Qui fait    le babysitting         chez toi?*
            *la cuisine*
            *les courses*
            *le jardinage*
            *le ménage*
            *la vaisselle*

*Qui      lave la voiture?*
         *promène le chien?*
         *range la chambre?*

*Moi*

*Ma mère*

*Mon père*

*Ma sœur*

*Mon frère*

*Que fais-tu?*

*Je fais . . .*

*Je . . .*

## Activities

- Worksheets Set 1

- Miming activities

- Matching games

- Pairwork – information gap, Worksheet Set 2, 3

- Making picture and caption display

- Listening to **who** does **what**. Worksheet Set 3, 3

- Singing: make up a rap or use a well-known tune for household tasks

- Song

## Resources

- Worksheets Set 1, 1–4, Set 2, 1–3

- Worksheet Set 3, 3, made-up with household tasks

- Household task flashcards

- Made-up wordsearch, template 4b

- Pelmanism – household tasks words and pictures, template 1

- Cards for sentence-building

- Noughts and crosses, templates 3a and 3b, and small OHT pictures

- Cue cards

- Any appropriate props

- Song cassette

## Assignments

Pictures and cassette describing own family's division of household tasks,
with sound effects made by pupils' use of props and voices, etc.

*LE FRANÇAIS, C'EST FACILE!*

# Module 6 At home

# Topic (iv) At the table

## Topic
(iv) At the table

## Communicative objective
Coping at mealtimes

## Linguistic objectives (examples)

*Sur la table*

*Mets:* use appropriate numbers
  *une assiette*
  *un couteau*
  *une cuiller*
  *une fourchette*
  *une serviette*
  *un verre*

*Passe-moi . . . s'il te plaît*

Food vocabulary

*Voilà*

*Merci*

*Tu veux . . .?*

*Oui, s'il te plaît*

*Non, merci*

*Encore du pain?*

*Tu aimes ça?*

*Oui, c'est délicieux*

*Non, merci*

*Tu mets la table s.t.p.? Oui*

*Je mets la table? Oui s.t.p.*

## Activities
- Laying the table:
  - present vocabulary with objects if possible
  - pupils take turn in placing correct objects, then number of objects, on table
- Make wall display
- Speaking/writing *Sur la table il y a* revising numbers and new vocabulary
- Group lay table, one member does commentary
- Revision of food – likes/dislikes, Worksheet Set 2, 4 (keep to positive comments for politeness here)
- Practise questions and answers
- Noughts and crosses
- Beetle
- Kim's game
- Bingo – laid table

## Resources
- Food flashcards
- Table setting flashcards
- Noughts and crosses, templates 3a and 3b
- Beetle, template 1 (sets of place settings)
- Kim's game – table laid
- Bingo template B10

- Paper/plastic tableware
- Empty food packets, etc.
- Cut-out magazine pictures of food
- Real French food

## Assignments
Classroom display of table laid ready for meal

A real or simulated mealtime situation

# Module 6: At home

## 6(i) Family hobbies

- Use the flashcards from 2(i) to revise the members of the family.
- When presenting the hobbies use flashcards and use the *je* form initially.
- Question and answer with the flashcards will, therefore, be *Que fais-tu? Je . . .*; also show card and say *Tu regardes la télé?* The answer may be *Oui/Non* depending on the card shown; gradually elicit whole sentence instead of just *Oui/Non*.
- The worksheets Set 1, should also be completed using the first person only.
- Because of the length of whole sentences, a wordsearch would need to have the verbs e.g. *bricole*, and the nouns e.g. *la voiture* separately; a follow-up activity could then be to link up appropriate verbs and nouns.
- Family flashcards or name cards can now be used to talk about what other people do.
- The double boxes of the Set 2 worksheets can be used to build sentences.
- Snap-sized cards with names, verbs and nouns could be given out for pupils to make up sentences about a make-believe family. To demonstrate understanding they can then draw or match pictures of these.
- Questions can now be used to encourage pupils to talk about their own family.
- A simple gap-filling pairwork exercise can be made using the snap template (1) cut in half. Pupils draw in two activities for themselves – through questions and answers they each fill in the two blanks and can then see if the two sets of cards match as they should.

**Note:** it has been decided not to teach the verbs using the infinitive because of the likely confusion once the verb is in use with *je, il, elle*.

### Assignment

- Using pictures of adverts from magazines (teenage ones are particularly useful) the pupils fill in blank speech bubbles to match pictures and make a display.
- A survey of family pastimes – the simplest format would be to set pastimes against family members, so pupils put ticks in boxes as they get information from each other; a graph could then be made of the most popular pastimes with particular family members.

## 6(ii) Meals

**Note:** it is **not** intended to introduce time fully here; it is a huge topic, fraught with problems for Special Needs pupils. However, four typical times of meals each day could be taught as items of vocabulary and simply used to clarify which meal is meant.

- Presentation of meals with simple times if desired.
- With the emphasis in this topic on **meals**, keep the food chosen to introduce/revise vocabulary appropriate to typical meals of your pupils, otherwise the vocabulary will become too large.
- Make good use of the Set 1 worksheets, wordsearch and bingo for the introduction and practice of this food vocabulary.
- The double worksheets (Set 2) are useful to link meal/place eaten, meal/food eaten.
- Again, with Kim's game, try to group foods typical to a particular meal to help pupils recognize meals and begin to categorize food in a different way from in Module 5.
- Pelmanism – if you use meal cards and food cards the game can be that the cards are only kept (won) if the food is appropriate to that meal. Encourage speaking during the game. Pupil 1: *le petit déjeuner* (as they turn it up). Pupil 2: *les frites – non, c'est le déjeuner.*
- Beetle too can have various groups of six cards to make up the possibilities for all four meals, so that pupils can then categorize the food under meals.

### Assignment

All of this important categorization of food can then be used to make a display of typical meals, with collage or drawings, with labels.

## 6(iii) Who does what?

- Beside the usual flashcard presentation and guessing games, mimes and props will give added interest and amusement here.
- Worksheets Set 1, then matching games, will reinforce the new vocabulary.
- A change from the usual listening activity could be to use sounds of activities for recognition – pupils can be encouraged to make the sound effects, with props, behind a screen/cupboard door.
- Noughts and crosses will encourage pupils to try to use the appropriate verb for the activity.
- The double worksheets, Set 2, can link family members to tasks and lead to speaking, reading or writing.
- An information gap pairwork exercise can be made using the above sheets by giving one pupil half A of the picture and the other half B of the sentence.

### Assignment

This is meant to be fun – but also a lot of useful social education is learnt here!

## 6(iv) At the table

- Present the vocabulary with objects if possible because this is a good opportunity for movement and for manipulating objects.
- Give plenty of opportunity for individuals or groups to lay a table – this revises recognizing numbers in a real situation too.
- Kim's game will help memorization.
- Noughts and crosses could be played flat on a table with pupils having to either say the correct item that is placed in a square or replace it with the correct cue card, or vice-versa.
- Beetle too can here get a new perspective with pupils actually building up their place-setting.
- At this stage the food items are mostly revised, although the class may be ready for some extra vocabulary to be presented. Use plastic food, empty packets, magazine pictures (on card and laminated if possible) and, of course, real French food if it is available and can be funded.
- *Passe-moi, Tu veux . . .?, Tu aimes . . .?, encore de . . .* should all be practised by pairs and groups with either pictures or realia to handle.

### Assignment

- The table laid for a meal can be a three-dimensional wall display using paper plates, plastic cutlery, etc. which can be glued or sellotaped on.
- The meal might be more feasible if done on a cross-curricular basis or in conjunction with the school canteen.

# MODULE 7 Looking after a visitor

## Timescale
1 term

## Areas of experience
A   B   C   E

## Topics | Communicative objectives

(i)   My family — Introducing a French visitor to members of the family

(ii)  My home — Showing a visitor around the home

(iii) Local facilities — Explaining what there is to do in the area

(iv)  Local transport — Discussing the best way of getting around

## Assignments
Plan of home with labels

Plan of town with facilities labelled

Design and make a poster to advertise a facility

Plan map showing routes/transport facilities

## Programme of study (part 1): Examples
Communicating in the target language

– take part in less structured role play

– ask for and give information

– copy sentences (and short texts)

## Cross-curricular opportunities
Designing and making — Design and Technology

Geography

Understanding the needs of others — PSE

## Opportunities for assessment
| | |
|---|---|
| Respond to flashcards | AT1:1; AT2:1,2 |
| Understand names of facilities | AT1:1 |
| Ask/answer questions about facilities | AT1:1,2; AT2:1,2,3 |
| Say what there is to do in a town | AT2:2,3 |
| Match words to pictures of facilities | AT3:1 |
| Label town plan | AT4:1 |
| Write simple sentences about what there is to do in a town | AT4:2,3 |

# Module 7 Looking after a visitor                    Topic (i) My family

## Topic
(i) My family

## Communicative objective
Introducing a French visitor to members of the family

## Linguistic objectives (examples)

*Voici*           *ma mère*
*Je te présente* *mon père*
                *ma sœur*
                *mon frère*
                *mon grand-père*
                *ma grand mère*
                • see teaching notes

*Voici mon chat*
        *chien*
        *lapin, etc.*

*Il/Elle s'appelle . . .*   • see teaching notes

*Bonjour*

*Ça va (?)*

*Enchanté*

## Activities
- Revision of family from Module 2
- Wordsearch
- Beetle (make up family)
- Role plays using other names
- Song

## Resources
- Ready-made wordsearch, template 4b
- Beetle (family), template 1
- Resources as for Module 2 for revision of family

---

- Props for dressing up
- Name cards for role plays (English first and surnames for English family as well as French name for visitor)
- Song cassette

## Assignments
Presentation of a short play showing a family meeting a French visitor

# Module 7 Looking after a visitor

# Topic (ii) My home

## Topic
(ii) My home

## Communicative objective
Showing a visitor around the home

## Linguistic objectives (examples)

*Voici  la chambre
        la chambre de mon frère
                    ma sœur
                    mes parents
        ma chambre
        ta chambre
        la cuisine
        la salle à manger
        la salle de bains
        le salon/le séjour
        les toilettes*

## Activities
- Flashcard/OHP games for revision – hiding/guessing/naming
- Matching games – snap, Pelmanism
- Beetle, rooms in the house
- Game – which room is missing? (OHT or cards)
- Pairwork guessing game with picture cards face down
- Worksheets Set 2, 1–2 for bedrooms belonging to members of the family
- Song

## Resources
- Worksheets Set 2, 1–2
- Flashcards – family
            rooms
- Bingo, template B6
- Beetle, template 1 (sets of rooms)
- Made-up wordsearch, template 4b
- OHT house and furniture
- Cue cards

- Cut-out pictures and labels
- Magazine pictures of rooms
- Song cassette

## Assignments
Plan or set of pictures of own home with room labels

Scene with visitor being shown around the home

# Module 7 Looking after a visitor     Topic (iii) Local facilities

### Topic
(iii) Local facilities

### Communicative objective
Explaining what there is to do in the area

### Linguistic objectives (examples)

*Qu'est-ce qu'il y a à Bath*
*à Plymouth?*

*À Plymouth il y a*   *un café*
       *un centre de sports*
       *un cinéma*
       *une disco(thèque)*
       *des magasins*
       *un musée*
       *un parc*
       *une patinoire*
       *une piscine*
       *une plage*
       *un port*

*Tu veux y aller?*

*Oui, s'il te plaît (or Je veux bien)*

*Non merci (or Je n'aime pas ça)*

*Je préfère . . .*

*On y va?*

### Activities
- Flashcard/OHP games
- Matching activities/games
- Worksheets Set 1, 1–4, Set 3, 1–2
- Worksheets Set 2 linking town and facility
- Miming
- Labelling town plan
- Look for information in French brochures
- Interpret information for French visitor in English
- Write simple sentences about what there is in a town
- Bingo with town outline and facilities
- Song
- IT opportunity

### Resources
- Worksheets Set 1, 1–4, Set 2, 1–2, Set 3, 1–2
- Town flashcards
- Bingo, template B9
- Pelmanism/snap, template 1
- Dominoes, template 2
- Town plan and pictures to glue on, template B9
- Cue cards

- Brochures from French towns (or English brochures to explain to French visitors)
- Song cassette

### Assignments
Plan of town with facilities labelled

Brochure to advertise a town

Poster to advertise a facility in the town

Make a tape about the facilities in your town to help blind tourists

# Module 7 Looking after a visitor

# Topic (iv) Local transport

● ● ● ● ● ● ● ● ● ● ● ● ● ● ● ● ● ● ● ● ● ● ● ● ● ● ● ● ● ● ● ● ● ● ● ● ●

### Topic
(iv) Local transport

### Communicative objective
Discussing the best way of getting around

### Linguistic objectives (examples)

*On va à (Andover)?*
*au cinéma?*
*à la piscine?*

*Oui, comment?*

*On prend l'autobus*
*le train*

*On y va à pied*
*à vélo*

*D'accord*

### Activities
- Flashcards, etc. to revise known transport words and present new ones
- Pairwork questions and answers using place and transport cards face down
- Role play
- Song

### Resources
- Worksheets Set 2, 1–3 linking places and transport
- Transport flashcards also from 5(i)
- Pictures and words for sentence-building
- Cue cards

- Large town plan
- Toy vehicles to use with the above if possible
- Song cassette

### Assignments
Role play deciding what to do and how to get there, linking 7(iii) and 7(iv)

● ● ● ● ● ● ● ● ● ● ● ● ● ● ● ● ● ● ● ● ● ● ● ● ● ● ● ● ● ● ● ● ● ● ● ● ●

# Module 7: Looking after a visitor

## 7(i) My family

- Revise family members using resources from Module 2.
- If required, for children from split families, it may be useful to have the following available: *mon beau-père, ma belle-mère* for step-parents, *mon demi-frère, ma demi-sœur* for half-brothers/sisters.
- Games like beetle and a wordsearch will also help to revise vocabulary.

**Assignment**

- Groupwork for role play: a French visitor being introduced into a British home – have props and name cards to complete the simulation.
- If a video is available to film the play, this would be a wonderful motivation.

**Note:** if pupils cannot manage *Il/Elle s'appelle*, they can say *ma mère s'appelle*, etc.

## 7(ii) My home

- Again, this is largely revision of 4(iii), so use a variety of activities to revise rooms in the house.
- Family flashcards and name cards are needed to present *la chambre de . . .* This can be practised with the double-box worksheets Set 2, 1–2.

**Assignment**

- The assignments are such that the scene suggested can build on the one in 7(i), and the set of labelled pictures may be done by pupils who find the concept of a plan too difficult.

## 7(iii) Local facilities

- As a new and significant set of vocabulary, these words must be thoroughly, but only gradually, presented and practised.
- Worksheets Set 1, wordsearch, bingo and matching games will reinforce vocabulary.

- Double-box worksheets (set 2) will encourage sentences: *À* (town) *il y a . . .*
- A large town plan can gradually be built up as a display with places being added as they are learnt.
- The thrill of just looking at brochures from France is a good enough reason for sending off to various towns in France, but they will also extend reading skills with truly (and obviously) authentic materials.
- Even British brochures with town plans and descriptions will be interesting and will allow some simple interpreting to take place.

**Assignments**

- This topic really lends itself to projects of various kinds. Posters and brochures can be individual or pair work; the town plan could involve a whole group; and the cassette could be spoken by one pupil and scripted by others.

## 7(iv) Local transport

- Revise known transport words from 5(i) and present new ones.
- Use but do not try to teach *à la, au, aux*. Some pupils will grasp it occasionally, but there is time in KS4 for this kind of development of grammar.
- If you can make a table town plan and use toy cars, buses, etc. this whole section comes to life!
- Encourage the simple dialogue by giving out place and transport Pelmanism cards and as each pair are turned up pupil 1 says *On va à la piscine* and pupil 2, etc. *Oui, on prend l'autobus* replies.
- Develop this by pupil 2 also having to pick up a place and say *Non, je préfère le cinéma*, etc.

**Assignment**

The role play will have been developed through the preceding activities.

# MODULE 8 Enjoying life

## Timescale
1 term

## Areas of experience
A   B

## Topics / Communicative objectives

| Topics | Communicative objectives |
|---|---|
| (i) Favourite pastimes | Understanding and naming sports and hobbies |
| (ii) Sports and hobbies | Exchanging information about sports and hobbies |
| (iii) Parts of the body | Understanding and naming parts of the body |
| (iv) Health | Asking and answering questions about personal health |

## Assignments
Design and make a poster advertising a sport/hobby

Survey/database of class interests

Exercise routine with instructions in French, maybe with a video

Collage – body and labels using cut-up magazines

Learn to play *boules*

## Programme of study (part 1): Examples
Communicating in the target language

– discuss own interests and compare them with those of others

– conduct surveys

## Cross-curricular opportunities

| | |
|---|---|
| Designing and making | Design and Technology |
| Me (my body and how it works) | PSE |
| Database work | } Maths |
| Measuring and graph work | |

## Opportunities for assessment

| | |
|---|---|
| Respond to flashcards | AT1:1; AT2:1 |
| Understand names of hobbies/sports | AT1:1 |
| Understand other people's opinions on hobbies/sports | AT1:1,2,3 |
| Ask/answer questions on hobbies/sports | AT1:1,2; AT2:1,2 |
| Ask/answer survey questions | AT1:2; AT2:1,2,3 |
| Say what your hobbies are | AT2:2,3 |
| Match words and pictures of hobbies/sports/body parts | AT3:1,2 |
| Follow written instructions to cut out and make body | AT3:2,3,4 |
| Label pictures | AT4:1,2 |
| Complete/write speech bubbles | AT4:1,2,3 |

# Module 8 Enjoying life

# Topic (i) Favourite pastimes

### Topic
(i) Favourite pastimes

### Communicative objective
Understanding and naming sports and hobbies

### Linguistic objectives (examples)
*le badminton*

*le basket*

*le cinéma*

*la cuisine*

*le cyclisme*

*le dessin*

*la disco(thèque)*

*l'équitation*

*le football*

*le jardinage*

*la musique*

*le rugby*

*les sports*

*la télé(vision)*

*le tennis*

*Tu aimes . . . ?*

*Oui, j'aime ça*

*Non, je n'aime pas ça*

### Activities
- Flashcard activities
- Worksheets Set 1, 1–4
- Worksheets Set 2, 1–4, linking sports and hobbies to preferences
- Miming
- Matching games – snap, Pelmanism, dominoes
- Noughts and crosses
- Playing *boules*
- Picture profile of likes/dislikes

### Resources
- Worksheets Set 1, 1–4, Set 2, 1–4
- Sports/hobbies flashcards
- Pelmanism/snap, template 1
- Dominoes, template 2
- Noughts and crosses, templates 3a and 3b
- Made-up wordsearch, template 4b
- Blank wordsearch, template 4a
- Likes/dislikes sheet, template 9
- Cue cards

- Set of plastic *boules*

### Assignments
Poster advertising sport or hobby

Learning to play *boules*

A labelled picture profile of personal interests

*LE FRANÇAIS, C'EST FACILE!*

# Module 8 Enjoying life

# Topic (ii) Sports and hobbies

● ● ● ● ● ● ● ● ● ● ● ● ● ● ● ● ● ● ● ● ● ● ● ● ● ● ● ● ● ● ● ● ●

## Topic
(ii) Sports and hobbies

## Communicative objective
Exchanging information about sports and hobbies

## Linguistic objectives (examples)

| | |
|---|---|
| *Que fais-tu* | *le weekend?* |
| | *le soir?* |
| *Je joue* | *au football* |
| | *au rugby* |
| | *au tennis* |
| | *au basket* |
| | *au badminton* |
| *Je fais* | *de l'équitation* |
| | *du cyclisme* |
| | *le dessin* |
| | *la cuisine* |
| | *le jardinage* |
| *Tu joues au . . . ?* | *Oui* |
| | *Non* |

*[Je joue . . .*
*Je ne joue pas . . .]*

| | |
|---|---|
| *Tu fais . . . ?* | *Oui* |
| | *Non* |

*[Je fais . . .*
*Je ne fais pas . . .]*

| | |
|---|---|
| *Je vais* | *au cinéma* |
| | *à la disco* |
| *J'aime* | *le sport* |
| | *la musique* |
| | *la télé* |

*Quel sport/passe-temps préfères-tu?*

*Je préfère . . .*

## Activities
- Worksheets Set 1, 1–4 and Set 2 – linking which activities take place when, or preferences
- Worksheets Set 3 – listening for activities/preferences
- Flashcard activities
- Matching games
- Miming/guessing games
- Survey
- Pairwork
- Taped profile of each pupil's own interests
- Sentence-building
- Song

## Resources
- Worksheets Set 1, 1–4, Set 2, 1–3, Set 3, 1–3
- Activity flashcards
- Pelmanism/snap, template 1
- Dominoes, template 2
- Noughts and crosses, templates 3a and 3b
- Made-up wordsearch, template 4b
- Survey, template 10
- Cue cards

- Cut-up syllable/sentence cards
- Blank cassettes
- Song cassette

## Assignments
Survey of class preferences for hobbies or sports

Make a cassette

● ● ● ● ● ● ● ● ● ● ● ● ● ● ● ● ● ● ● ● ● ● ● ● ● ● ● ● ● ● ● ● ●

# Module 8 Enjoying life

# Topic (iii) Parts of the body

## Topic
(iii) Parts of the body

## Communicative objectivee
Understanding and naming parts of the body

## Linguistic objectives (examples)

*La tête* – see 2(iii)
   *les dents*
   *les oreilles*
   *les yeux*

*le corps*
   *le bras*
   *le doigt*
   *le dos*
   *le genou*
   *la gorge*
   *la jambe*
   *la main*
   *le pied*

*Baissez/Baisse* . . .

*Levez/Lève* . . .

*Touchez/Touche* . . .

## Activities
- Recognition practice games:
  - point and say
  - *Simon dit*
- Exercising – see teaching notes page 156
- Worksheets Set 1, 1–4
- Beetle
- Make own wordsearch
- Following instructions to cut out parts of body or choose ready-made cut-outs
- Song
- IT opportunity

## Resources
- Worksheets Set 1, 1–4
- Body flashcards
- Pelmanism/snap/beetle, template 1
- Dominoes, template 2
- Noughts and crosses, templates 3a and 3b
- Made-up wordsearch, template 4b
- Blank wordsearch, template 4a
- Bingo, template B12
- Cue cards

- Magazines to cut up
- Song cassette

## Assignments
Collage – body and labels using cut-up magazine pictures

Exercise routine in French (possibly using keyboard rhythm or well-known tune)

# Module 8 Enjoying life

# Topic (iv) Health

**Topic**

(iv) Health

**Communicative objective**

Asking and answering questions about personal health

**Linguistic objectives (examples)**

*Ça va?*

*Oui, ça va bien*

*Non, ça ne va pas*

*Comme ci, comme ça*

*J'ai mal  à la tête*
       *aux dents*
       *aux oreilles*
       *aux yeux*
       *au bras*
       *au doigt*
       *au dos*
       *au genou*
       *à la gorge*
       *à la jambe*
       *à la main*
       *au pied*

**Activities**

- Presentation of *J'ai mal . . .*
- Mimes of pains
- Labelling pictures*
- Completing speech bubbles*
- Sticking plasters (on picture) to show where pain is*

*Combination of these will make classroom display

**Resources**

- Worksheets Set 2, 1–3
- Body flashcards
- *J'ai mal* flashcard
- Speech bubbles, template 7

- Pictures or photographs of people

**Assignments**

Classroom display (humorous?) of ailments, e.g. set out as a doctor's waiting room queue

# Module 8: Enjoying Life

## 8(i) Favourite pastimes

- Flashcard presentation of vocabulary (nouns only).
- Link words with pictures using cue cards and the worksheets Set 1.
- Matching games to reinforce new vocabulary, see Module 3(ii).
- Re-introduce likes and dislikes to give opportunity for questions and answers between pupils and teachers, and pairwork.
- Pupils can now build up a personal profile of their likes and dislikes using the appropriate sheets or designing their own.
- This will then be a stimulus for oral and written work.
- Making up a wordsearch after completing a prepared wordsearch adds yet more individuality.
- The suggested posters, suitably labelled, can serve as a classroom display, and, therefore, provide reinforcement of the vocabulary for the rest of the module.

### Assignment
- Labelled picture profile can make use of the like/dislike sheets.
- Pupils could learn to play *boules* while others are doing other assignments.

## 8(ii) Sports and hobbies

- Extend the exchange of information by introducing the appropriate verbs to give the action rather than just the noun – show this by miming.
- There will need to be plenty of practice to reinforce the different verbs – there will initially be confusion between them but remember it is the message that counts!
- Questions: at first accept *oui/non* answers and only gradually elicit the fuller answers using the appropriate verb.

### Assignment
- The survey can be a small group rather than the whole class, to make it more manageable. Pupils will need to fill in the names of the people in the group and the sports/activities chosen for the survey. Some could survey sports and some other activities to further authentically limit the size of the survey.
- The cassette could be either an interview (pairwork) or an individual oral profile of interests.

## 8(iii) Parts of the body

- Basic activities are as in the introduction for the presentation of new vocabulary.
- Playing *Simon dit* is a fun, active way of involving the pupils in the word recognition.

### Assignment
- From *Simon dit*, simple exercise routines can be built up. Pupils could work on individual routines, using keyboard rhythms or well-known tunes.
- Cut-outs from magazines – pupils can either be free to cut out the pictures they need to build up their collage person or directions can be given to guide them, e.g. *découpez un bras*, etc.
- When the collages are made they can be labelled and the display will reinforce vocabulary for the next topic.
- Both parts of the assignment have been gradually built up during the topic.

## 8(iv) Health

- Use mime and facial expression to present *J'ai mal*.
- Pupils can come out in front of the class in groups to mime the doctor's waiting-room queue and the rest of class say the words.
- Using a packet of cheap sticking plasters, pupils put a plaster on a picture and give the appropriate utterance.
- This can become a written exercise if they then complete speech bubbles to go with each picture.

**Note:** teachers can introduce *J'ai mal à la/au/aux*, but so long as pupils are communicating, there is no need at this level to labour such grammatical points. Pupils should, however, when writing from a cue, copy the above correctly.

### Assignment
From the above activities a queue of people (cut-outs or drawings) with their ailments can make a humorous classroom display.

# MODULE 9 Being a teenager

● ● ● ● ● ● ● ● ● ● ● ● ● ● ● ● ● ● ● ● ● ● ● ● ● ● ● ● ● ● ● ● ● ● ● ● ● ● ● ●

## Timescale
1 term

## Areas of experience
A    D

## Topics / Communicative objectives

| Topics | Communicative objectives |
|---|---|
| (i) Pocket money | Exchanging information about how money is earned |
| (ii) Spending my money | Exchanging information about how money is spent |
| (iii) Clothes | Understanding and naming common items of clothing |

## Assignments
Survey on spending habits

– Poster

– Scrapbook — this module allows the opportunity for an end of Key Stage

– Tape — creative product; ideally, individuals or groups work on their

– Montage — selected project connected with how they spend their money

– Magazine

## Programme of study (part 1): Examples
Communicating in the target language

– describe everyday activities

– discuss own interests and compare them with those of others

– work with authentic materials

Developing cultural awareness:

– conduct surveys

## Cross-curricular opportunities

| | |
|---|---|
| Money | Maths |
| Myself, my needs, how I spend my money | PSE |

## Opportunities for assessment: Examples

| | |
|---|---|
| Respond to flashcards | AT1:1, AT2:1 |
| Understand names of clothes | AT1:1 |
| Understand how other people spend their money | AT1:2,3 |
| Ask/answer questions on spending | AT1:1,2; AT2:1,2 |
| Ask/answer survey questions | AT1:1,2; AT2:1,2,3 |
| Say how you spend money | AT2:2,3 |
| Matching words/pictures (clothes/leisure) | AT3:1,2 |
| Match pictures to description | AT3:1,2,3 |
| Label pictures | AT4:1,2 |
| Write a few sentences about picture/own spending | AT4:2,3 |

● ● ● ● ● ● ● ● ● ● ● ● ● ● ● ● ● ● ● ● ● ● ● ● ● ● ● ● ● ● ● ● ● ● ● ● ● ● ● ●

# Module 9 Being a teenager

# Topic (i) Pocket money

●●●●●●●●●●●●●●●●●●●●●●●●●●●●●●●●●●●●●●●●●●●●●●●

## Topic
(i) Pocket money

## Communicative objective
Exchanging information about how money is earned

## Linguistic objectives (examples)

*Combien d'argent de poche as-tu?*

*J'ai . . . livres*

*Il/Elle a . . . livres*

*On me donne . . . livres*

*Qu fais–tu pour gagner l'argent?*

*Je travaille  dans . . .*
              *pour . . .*

*J'aide à la maison* see 6(iii)

*Je livre les journaux*

*Je promène le chien*

*Je fais du babysitting*

Numbers (as appropriate)

## Activities
- Presentation with coins, numbers and flashcards
- Worksheets Set 1, 1–4
- OHP games/noughts and crosses
- Miming
- Matching words and pictures
- Counting money
- Song

## Resources
- Worksheets Set 1, 1–4
- Household task flashcards
- Number sheets
- Various flashcards linked with this topic
- Noughts and crosses, templates 3a and 3b, e.g. with jobs for pocket money
- French name cards, template 15
- Cue cards

- Number cards
- Imitation money
- Pictures of people
- Song cassette

## Assignments
The topic works towards the final assignment – see page 160

It could begin as a survey on how money is earned

●●●●●●●●●●●●●●●●●●●●●●●●●●●●●●●●●●●●●●●●●●●●●●●

# Module 9 Being a teenager

# Topic (ii) Spending my money

## Topic
(ii) Spending my money

## Communicative objective
Exchanging information about how money
is spent

## Linguistic objectives (examples)

*Que fais-tu avec l'argent?*

*Je vais   au cinéma*
*au club*
*à la disco*
*au match de foot*
*à la piscine*

*J'achète   les bonbons*
*les cassettes*
*les disques*
*les magazines*
*les vêtements*

*C'est cher*

*Ce n'est pas cher*

## Activities
- Flashcard presentation/games
- Matching cue cards
- Recognizing and saying prices
- Listening and matching prices to items, Worksheet Set 3, 3
- Choosing realistic prices for items, worksheet Set 1, 4
- Discussing dear/cheap
- Class survey
- Song

## Resources
- Worksheets Set 1, 4, Set 2, 1–3, Set 3, 3
- Various flashcards
- Made-up wordsearch, template 4b
- Noughts and crosses, templates 3a and 3b
- Pelmanism/snap, template 1
- Survey sheet, template 10
- Cue cards

- Price cards
- Song cassette

## Assignments
Survey on spending habits

# Module 9 Being a teenager

## Topic
(iii) Clothes

## Communicative objective
Understanding and naming common items of clothing

## Linguistic objectives (examples)

*un chapeau*

*des chaussettes*

*des chaussures*

*un chemisier*

*un collant*

*une cravate*

*une écharpe*

*un jean*

*une jupe*

*un pull*

*une robe*

*un short*

*un t-shirt*

*une veste*

*Il/Elle porte . . .*

Numbers 1–100

## Activities
- Flashcard presentation
- Building up outfits on OHT
- Worksheets Set 1, 1–4
- Wordsearch
- Matching games – matching prices to clothes, discussing if they are cheap or expensive
- Pupils say what a person in a magazine picture is wearing
- Matching pictures with descriptions
- Bingo – clothes in suitcase
- Song

## Resources
- Worksheets Set 1, 1–4
- Clothes flashcards
- Pelmanism/snap, template 1
- Dominoes, template 2
- Bingo, template B11
- Made-up wordsearch, template 4b
- OHT clothes, cut out from picture sheets
- Cue cards
- Number sheets, templates 16a and 16b

- Prices
- Clothes
- Magazine pictures of clothes
- Song cassette

## Assignments
Poster

Scrapbook

Tape

Montage

Magazine

this module allows the opportunity for an end of Key Stage creative product; ideally, individuals or groups work on their selected project connected with how they spend their money

Fashion show – pupils can introduce their own or each other's actual or ideal outfits

Ideal outfit and costing (not related to actual spending power). Ideal outfit could be drawn or made up from collage of magazine pictures

*LE FRANÇAIS, C'EST FACILE!*

# Module 9: Being a teenager

## 9(i) Pocket money

### How much? (money and numbers)
- Revise 1–20 in a variety of ways.
- Use plastic pound coins or tokens to give out and pupils say how much they have then: *Combien d'argent as-tu? J'ai . . .*
- Move on to how much pocket money they receive.
- French name cards or pictures from magazines could then be linked with amounts of money: *Il/Elle* (or name) *a . . . livres.*

### How much money is earned – vocabulary
- Present flashcards for how money is earned.
- Mimes can reinforce this vocabulary.
- Then Worksheets Set 1 and OHT noughts and crosses will give more practice.
- Sentence-building can be done on the board or OHP with pictures of people or their names, and amounts of money and speech bubbles for pupils to say how it is earned.

### How money is earned – exchange of information
- Initially teacher can ask question: *Tu livres les journaux?* with single *oui/non* response.
- Then go on to *Que fais-tu . . . ?* question encouraging a full answer.
- Then pairwork can be used to exchange information.

## 9(ii) Spending my money
- Revise the vocabulary for going to places.
- Introduce vocabulary for items purchased using flashcards/OHT, etc.
- Have price cards for pupils to say prices they see. Careful – you are here using **English** prices since pupils are shopping in England.
- A wordsearch will reinforce words.
- Noughts and crosses can be used to get pupils to put correct verbs, i.e. *Je vais/J'achète* with images given.

### Discussing prices
- Price activity as above.
- Price cards can be put with flashcards for pupils to learn *C'est cher/Ce n'est pas cher.*

- Worksheet Set 3, 3 can be made for pupils to listen for prices of items.
- Worksheets Set 2 will help pupils to write down information from hearing items and prices and could also be given with items and prices for pupils to comment in writing *C'est cher/Ce n'est pas cher*.
- Snap card sized pictures can be given out to pupils (four and five each) with an equal number of relevant prices to help them learn to put realistic prices on items.

### Assignment
- The suggested survey will give ample speaking/listening/recording practice in a realistic activity.

## 9(iii) Clothes
- Flashcard/cue card presentation of new vocabulary.
- OHT cut-outs can build up outfits.
- Worksheets Set 1 and wordsearch will reinforce vocabulary.
- Any of the matching games can be used here.
- Beetle will build up outfits; Kim's game will help memorize vocabulary.
- Magazine cut-outs can be used for pupils to list the clothes worn.
- Pupils can be given actual clothes to dress up in or simply to name. This could be followed by a 'silly fashion show' (or a serious one) with a commentary on what people are wearing.

### Price of clothes
- Higher numbers can be taught (60–100 included if pupils can cope with these).
- The same levels of activity as in 8(ii) can be done matching prices and clothes, discussing relative value for money, etc.

### Assignment
- The final assignment suggestion on clothes, with either cut-outs or pupils' own illustrations is a necessary alternative to discussions of money for those who receive little or none. The outfit can be costed so that the element of money is still included.

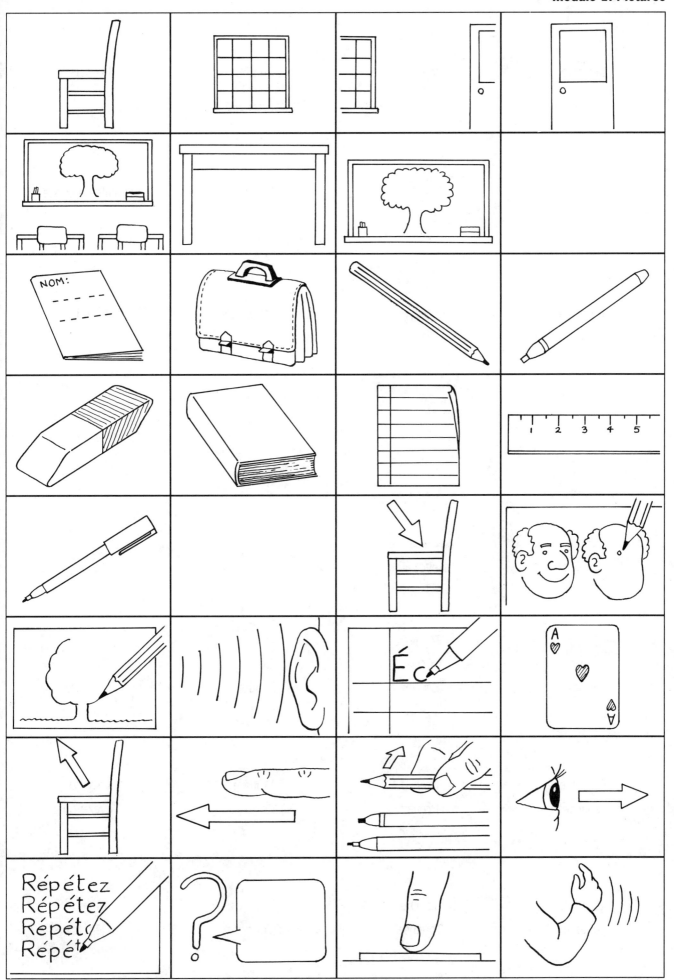

*LE FRANÇAIS, C'EST FACILE!*

## Module 1: Vocabulary

| | | | |
|---|---|---|---|
| la porte | le mur | la fenêtre | la chaise |
| | le tableau | la table | la salle de classe |
| le feutre | le crayon | le cartable | le cahier |
| la règle | le papier | le livre | la gomme |
| Copie<br>Copiez | Assieds-toi<br>Asseyez-vous | | le stylo |
| Joue<br>Jouez | Écris<br>Écrivez | Écoute<br>Écoutez | Dessine<br>Dessinez |
| Regarde<br>Regardez | Prends<br>Prenez | Montre<br>Montrez | Lève-toi<br>Levez-vous |
| Viens ici<br>Venez ici | Touche<br>Touchez | Réponds<br>Répondez | Répète<br>Répétez |

*LE FRANÇAIS, C'EST FACILE!*

| | | | |
|---|---|---|---|
| mon frère | ma sœur | mon père | ma mère |
| petit | grand | mon grand-père | ma grand-mère |
| les yeux | les cheveux | mince | gros |
| le chat | longs | frisés | courts |
| le hamster | le cochon d'Inde | le chien | le cheval |
| la souris | le serpent | le poisson rouge | le lapin |
| J'aime | Tu aimes? | | la tortue |
| Je préfère | Je déteste | J'adore | Je n'aime pas |

**Module 3: Vocabulary**

| | | | |
|---|---|---|---|
| le français | le drame<br>le théâtre | l'art<br>le dessin | l'anglais |
| les maths | l'informatique | l'histoire | la géographie |
| le sport | les sciences | la religion | la musique |
| | | | la technologie |
| difficile | facile | casse-pieds | amusant |
| | | moche | super |
| le matin | la récréation | le déjeuner | l'emploi du temps |
| | après | avant | l'après-midi |

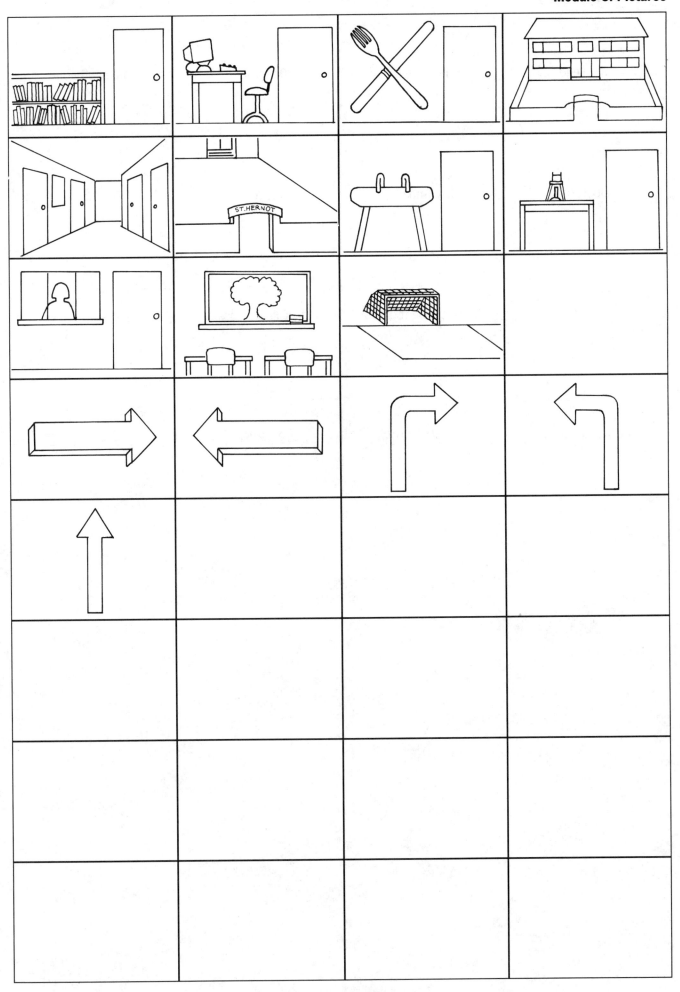

| | | | |
|---|---|---|---|
| le collège | la cantine | le bureau | la bibliothèque |
| le laboratoire | le gymnase | la cour | le couloir |
| | le terrain de football | la salle de classe | la réception |
| Tournez à gauche | Tournez à droite | à gauche | à droite |
| | | | Allez tout droit |
| | | | |
| | | | |
| | | | |

**Module 4: Vocabulary**

| | | | |
|---|---|---|---|
| la maison | le jardin | le garage | l'appartement |
| sur la côte au bord de la mer | à la campagne | dans un village | dans une ville |
| à Morlaix | à Plymouth | en France | en Angleterre |
| | | | à . . . |
| la pièce | l'escalier | la cuisine | la chambre |
| les toilettes | le salon le séjour | la salle de bains | la salle à manger |
| | | | |
| en face de | à côté de | au premier étage | au rez-de-chaussée |

*LE FRANÇAIS, C'EST FACILE!*

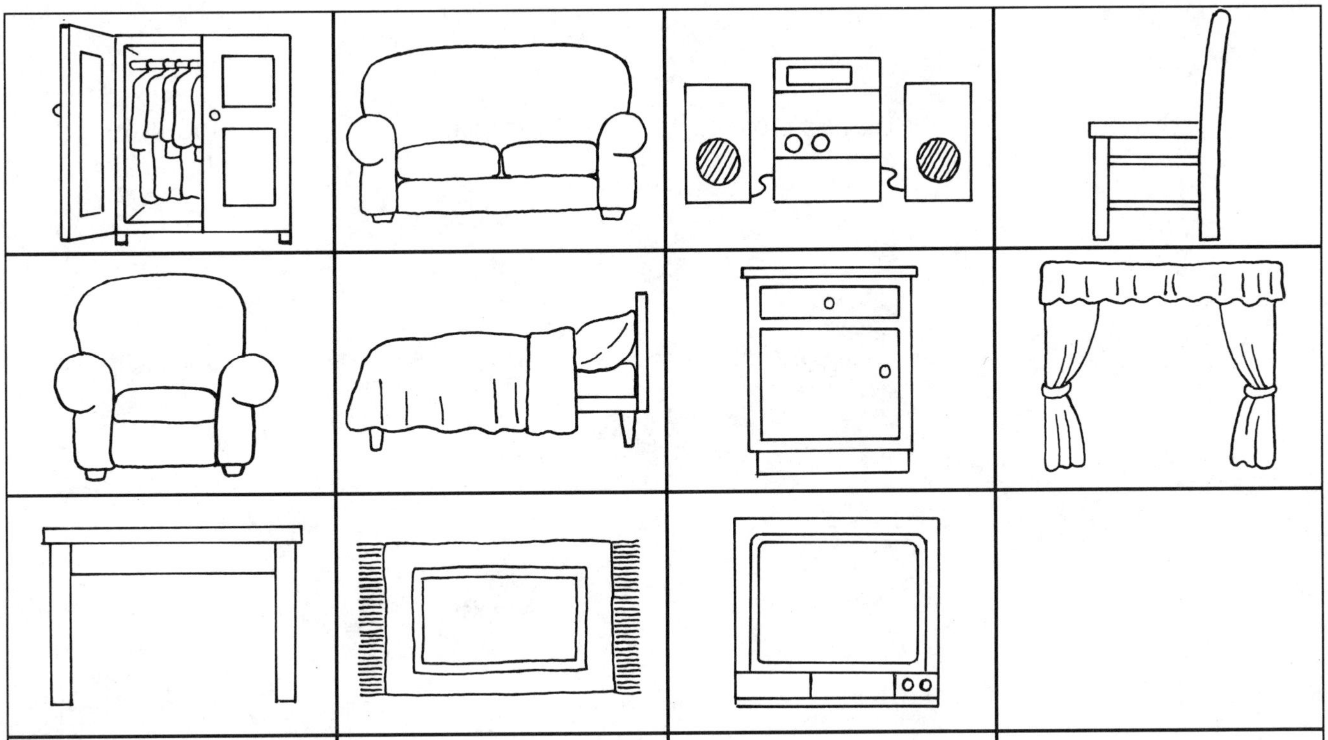

**Module 4: Vocabulary**

| | | | |
|---|---|---|---|
| la chaise | la chaîne-stéréo | le canapé | l'armoire |
| les rideaux | le placard | le lit | le fauteuil |
| | la télé(vision) | le tapis | la table |
| | | | |
| | | | |
| | | | |
| | | | |
| | | | |

*LE FRANÇAIS, C'EST FACILE!*

*LE FRANÇAIS, C'EST FACILE!*

**Module 5: Vocabulary**

| | | | |
|---|---|---|---|
| le train | le bateau<br>le ferry | l'avion | l'aéroglisseur |
| | | la voiture | le tunnel |
| | la Manche | La France | l'Angleterre |
| l'épicerie<br>l'alimentation | la charcuterie | la boulangerie | la boucherie |
| le marché | le magasin | le magasin | l'hypermarché |
| | | le tabac | le supermarché |
| les chips | les bonbons | le croissant | la baguette |
| la glace | le fromage | les frites | le chocolat |

*LE FRANÇAIS, C'EST FACILE!*

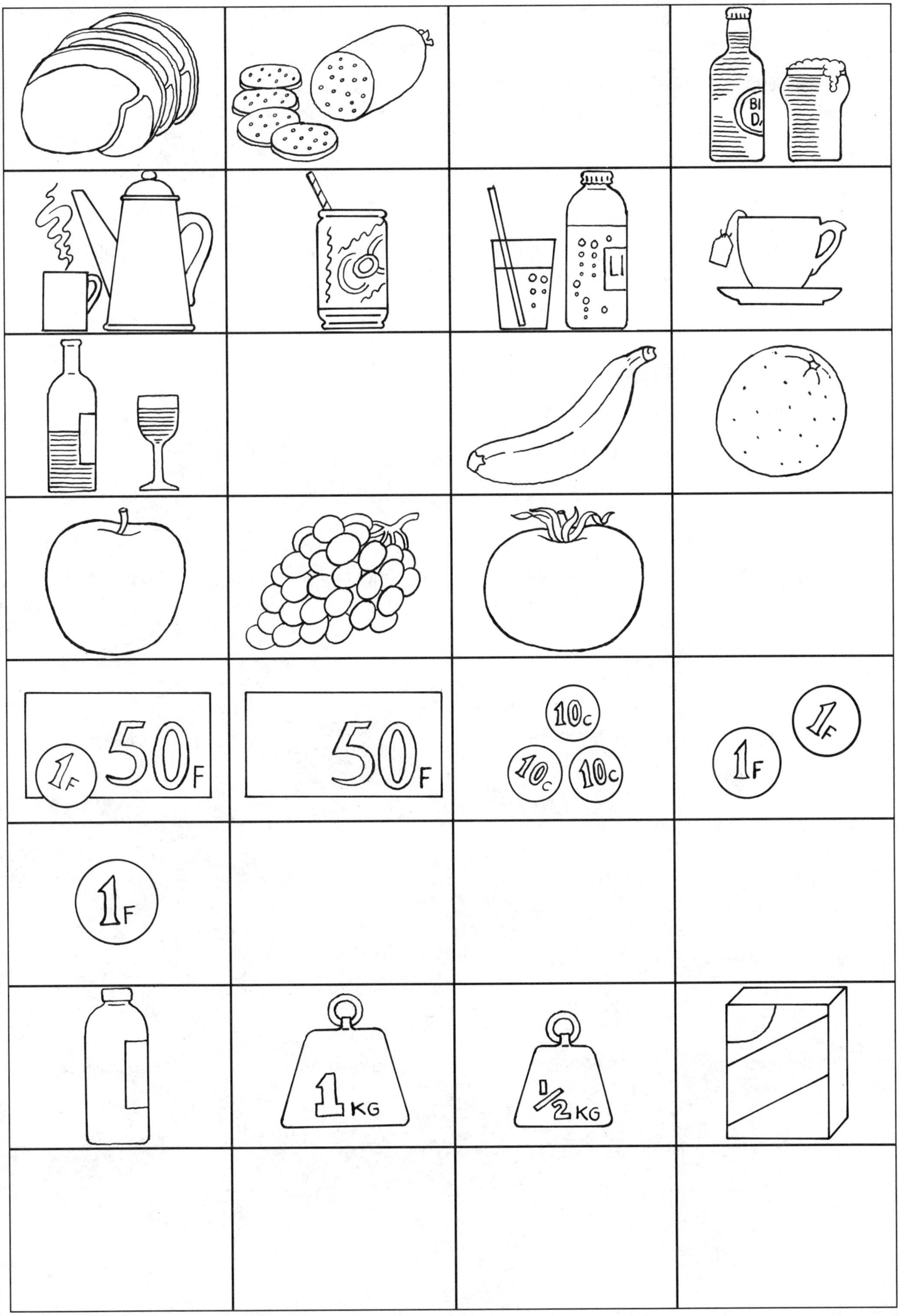
1F 50F
50F
10c
10c 10c
1F
1F
1F
1 KG
1/2 KG

**Module 5: Vocabulary**

| | | | |
|---|---|---|---|
| la bière | | le saucisson | le jambon |
| le thé | la limonade | le coca | le café |
| l'orange | la banane | | le vin |
| | la tomate | les raisins | la pomme |
| le franc | le centime | le billet (de 50 francs) | l'argent |
| | | | la pièce |
| un paquet de | un demi-kilo de | un kilo de | une bouteille de |
| | | | |

*LE FRANÇAIS, C'EST FACILE!*

| | | | |
|---|---|---|---|
| jouer avec des amis | jouer aux cartes | écouter la musique | bricoler |
| regarder la télé(vision) | regarder un magazine | regarder le journal | jouer avec l'ordinateur |
| | | | réparer la voiture |
| le dîner | le goûter | le déjeuner | le petit déjeuner |
| | | | devant la télé |
| les céréales | les carottes | les biscuits | le beurre |
| les gâteaux | l'eau minérale | le croque-monsieur | la confiture |
| le lait | le jus d'orange | le hot-dog | le hamburger |

*LE FRANÇAIS, C'EST FACILE!*

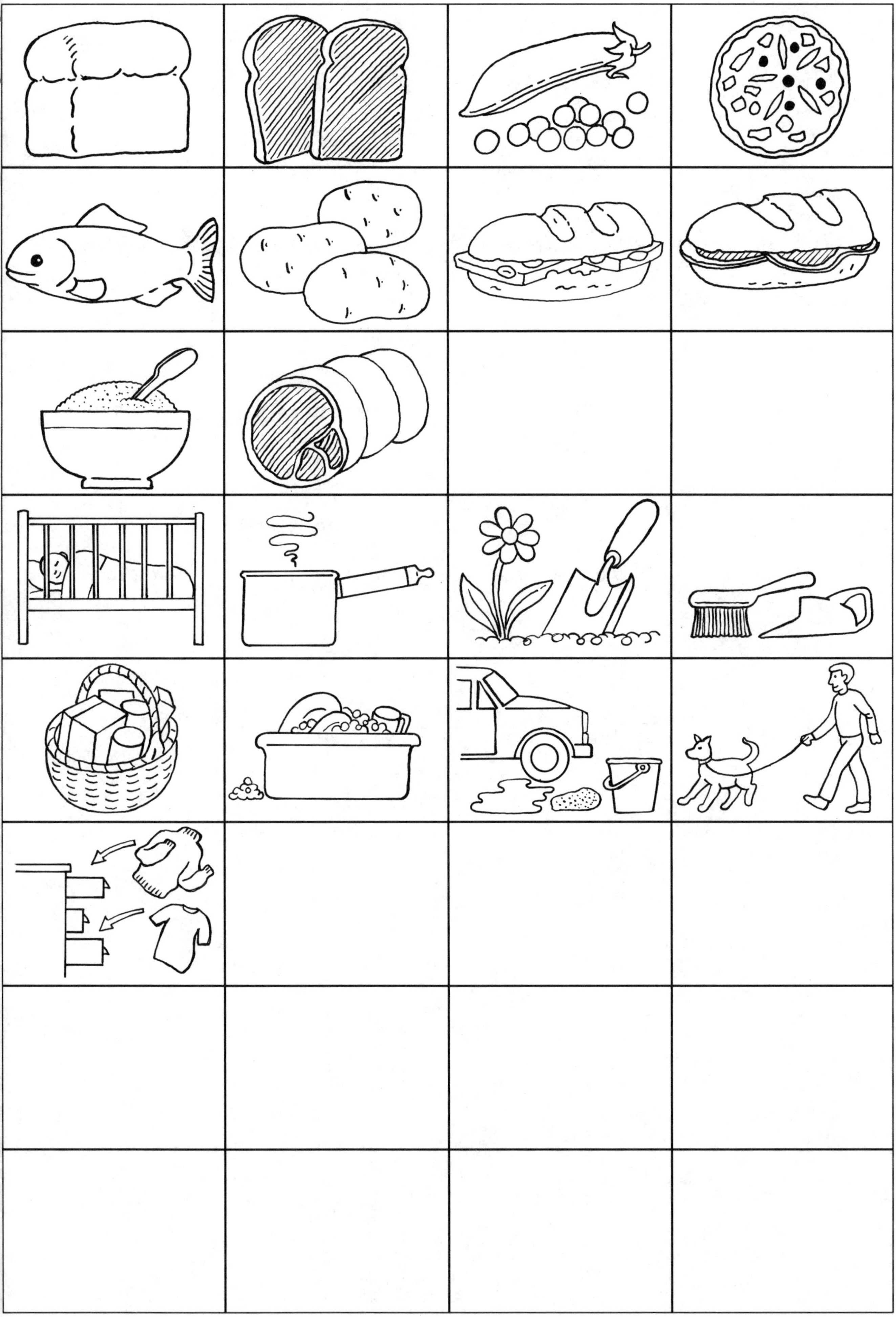

| | | | |
|---|---|---|---|
| la pizza | les petits pois | le pain grillé | le pain |
| le sandwich au jambon | le sandwich au fromage | les pommes de terre | le poisson |
| | | la viande | le sucre |
| faire le ménage | faire le jardinage | faire la cuisine | faire le babysitting |
| promener le chien | laver la voiture | faire la vaisselle | faire les courses<br>faire le shopping |
| ranger ma chambre | | | |
| | | | |
| | | | |

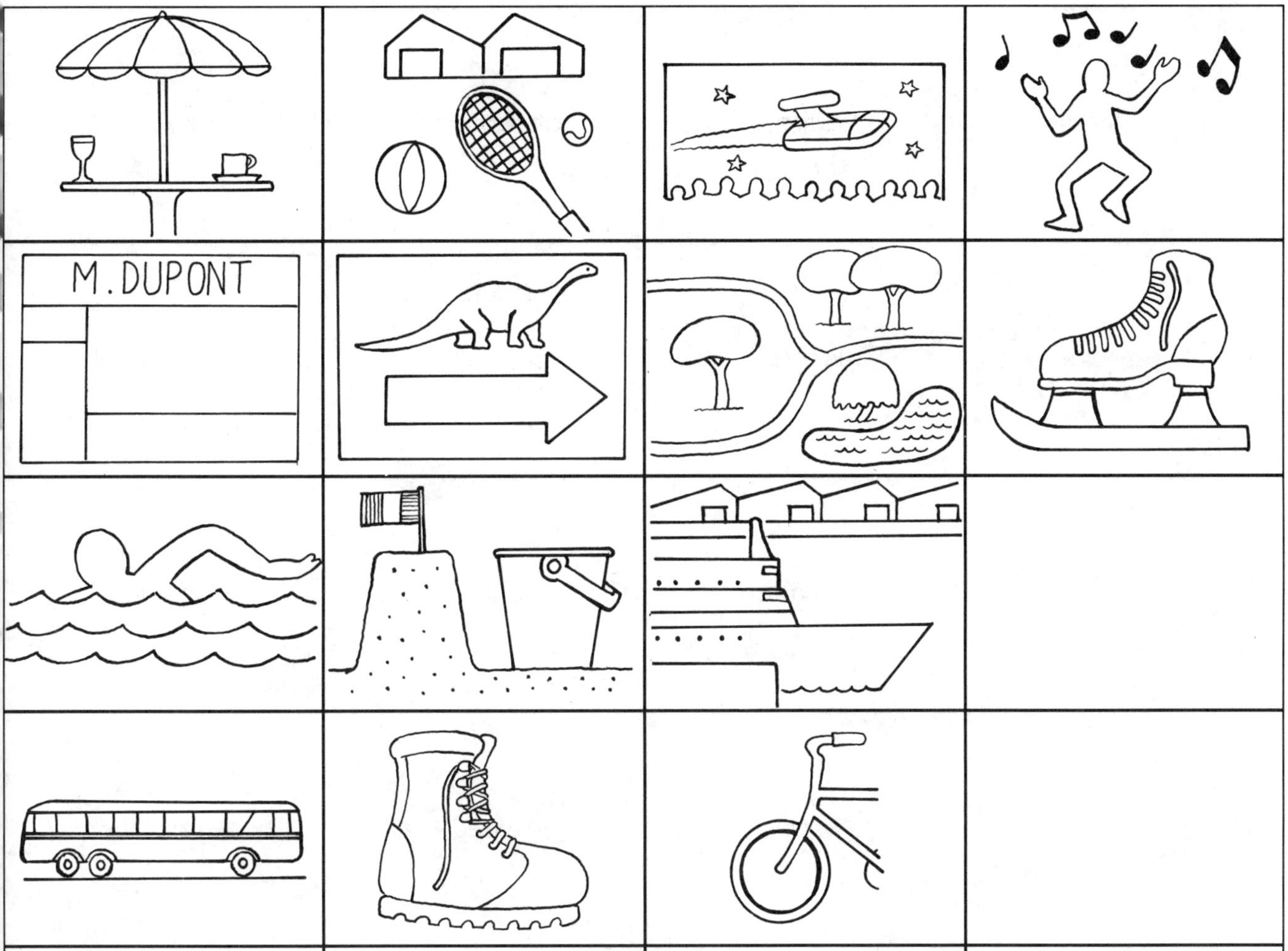
M.DUPONT

**Module 7: Vocabulary**

| | | | |
|---|---|---|---|
| la disco(thèque) | le cinéma | le centre de sports | le café |
| la patinoire | le parc | le musée | les magasins |
| | le port | la plage | la piscine |
| | à vélo | à pied | en autobus |
| | | | |
| | | | |
| | | | |
| | | | |

*LE FRANÇAIS, C'EST FACILE!*

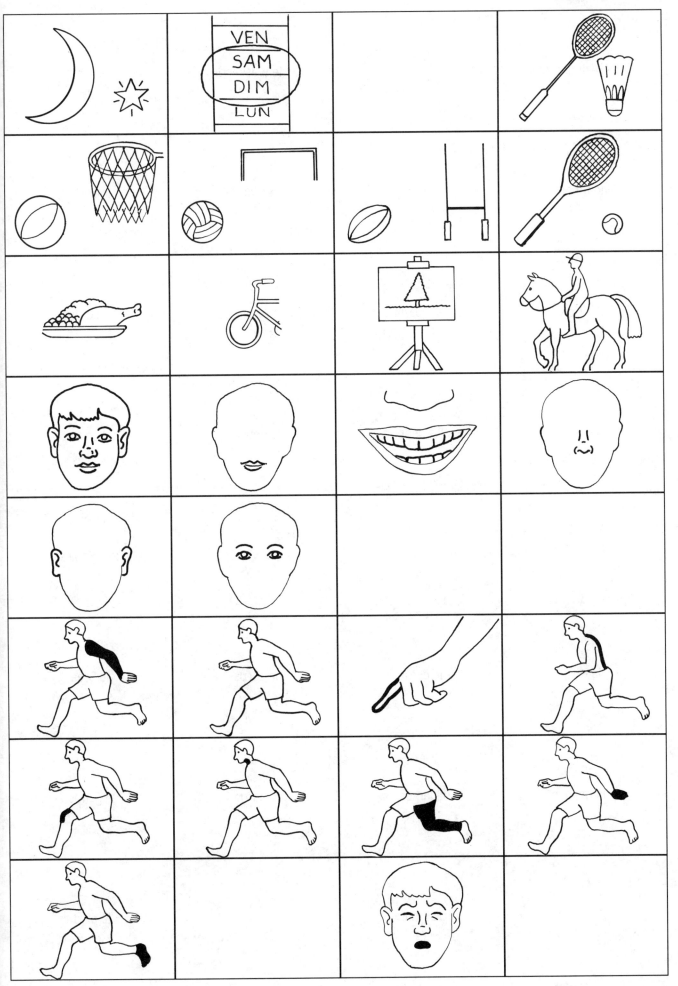

## Module 8: Vocabulary

| | | | |
|---|---|---|---|
| le badminton | | le weekend | le soir |
| le tennis | le rugby | le football | le basket |
| l'équitation | le dessin | le cyclisme | la cuisine |
| le nez | les dents | la bouche | la tête |
| | | les yeux | les oreilles |
| le dos | le doigt | le corps | le bras |
| la main | la jambe | la gorge | le genou |
| | J'ai mal | | le pied |

*LE FRANÇAIS, C'EST FACILE!*

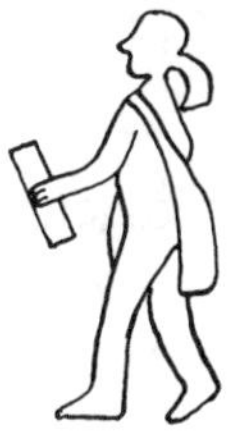
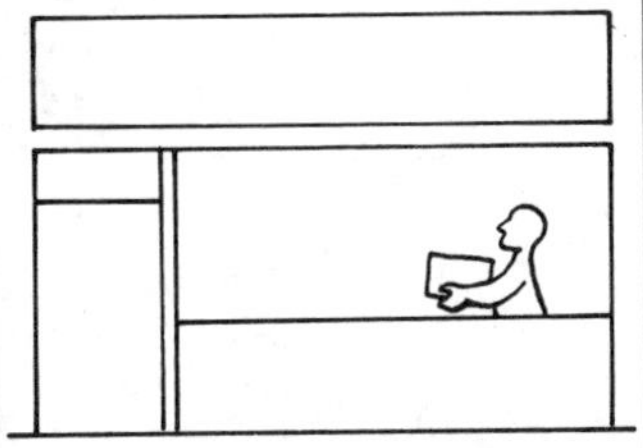
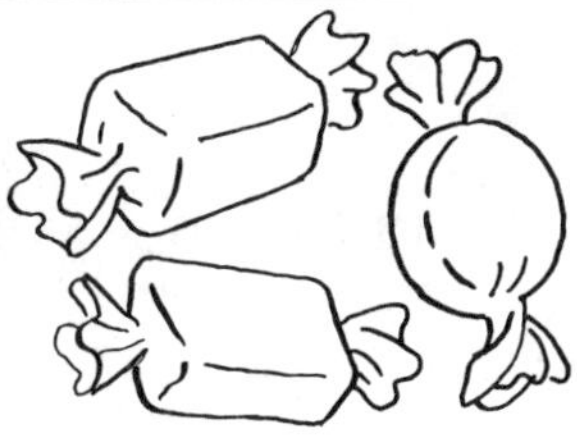
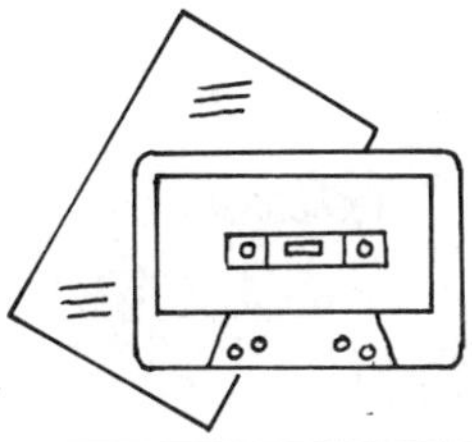
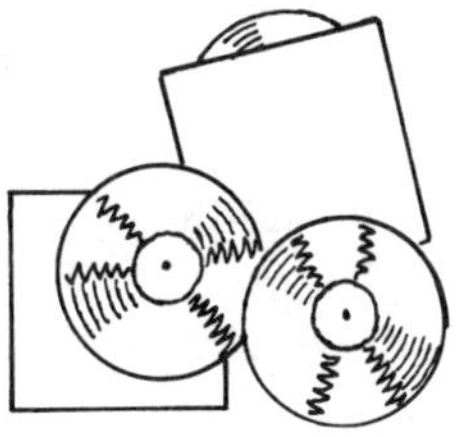
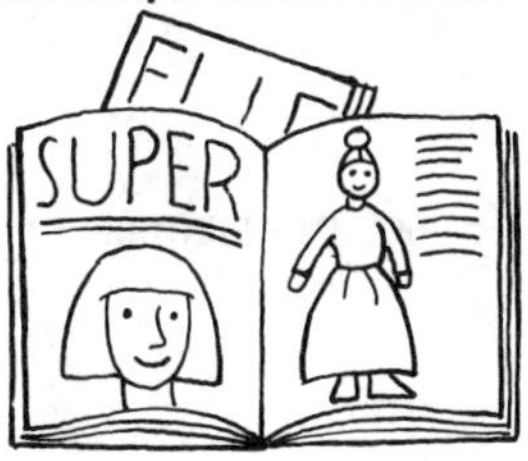
SUPER
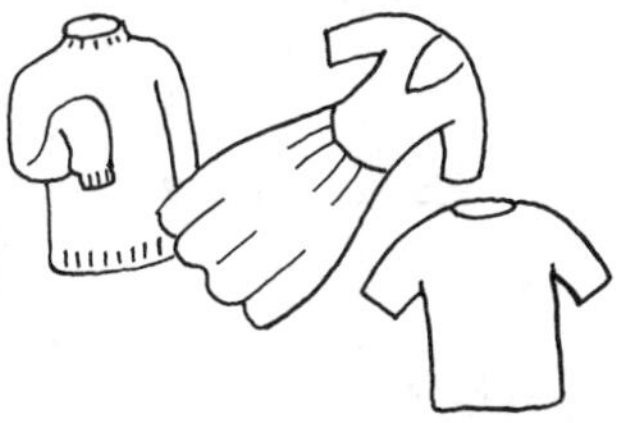
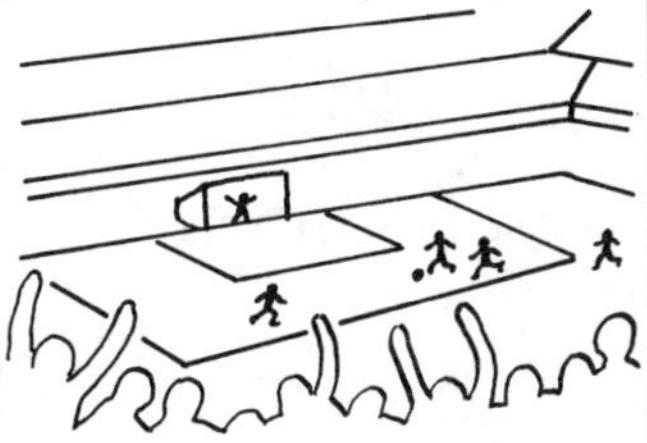
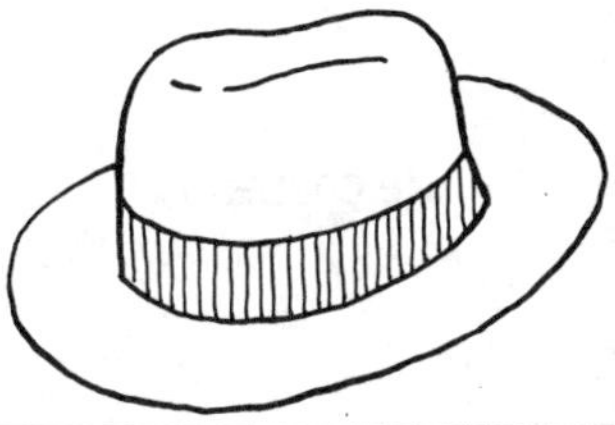
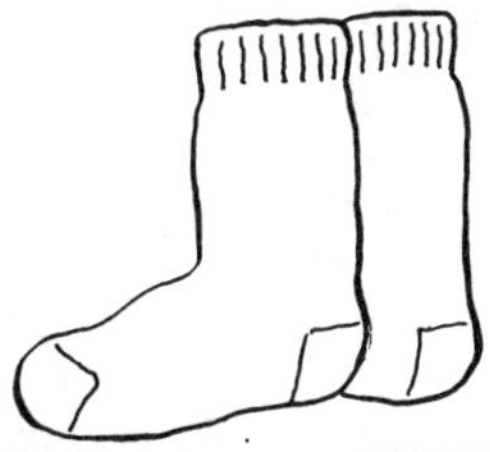
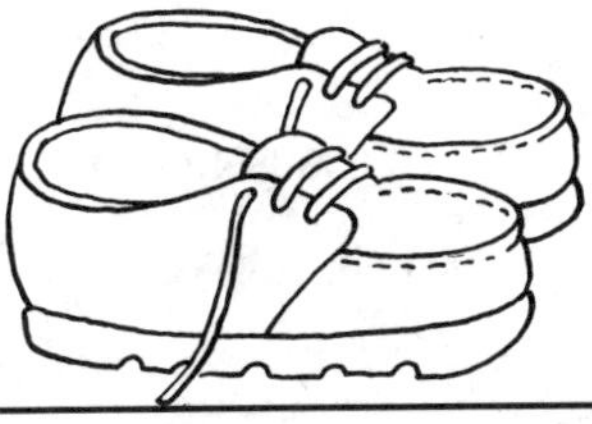
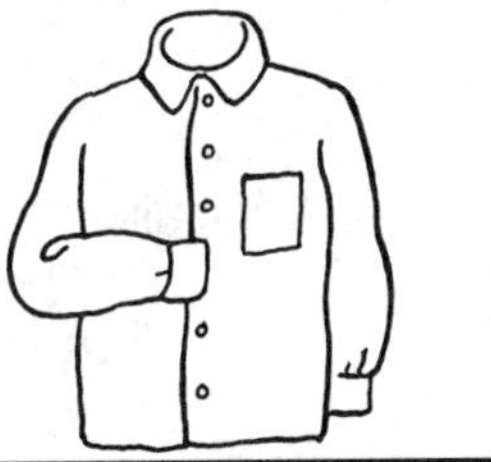
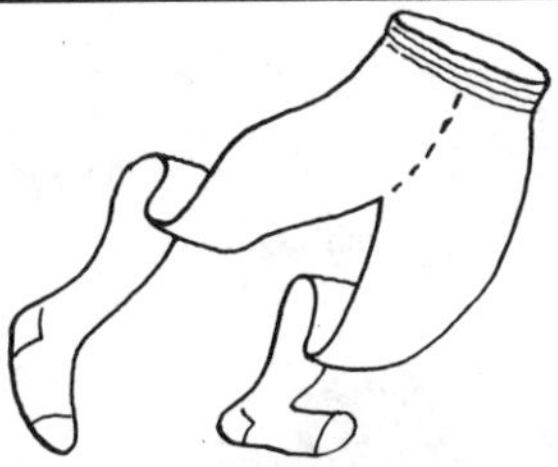
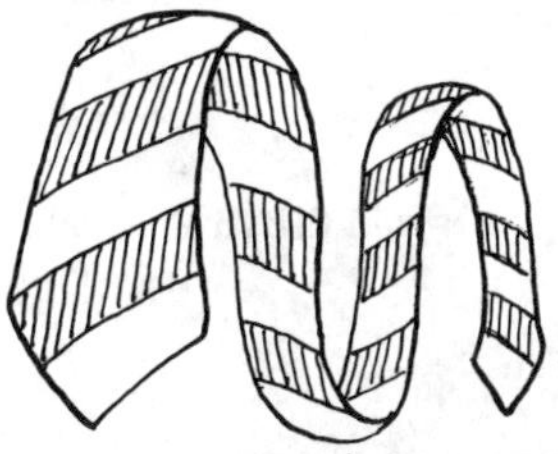
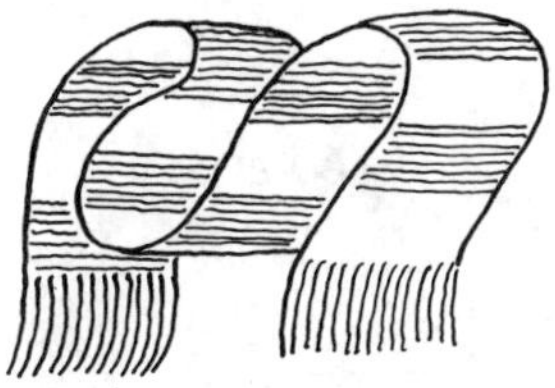
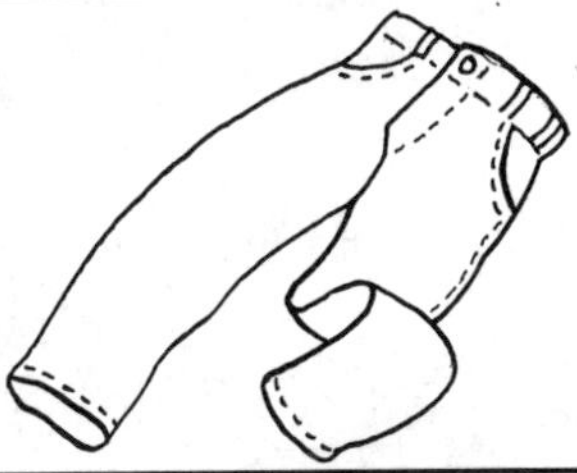
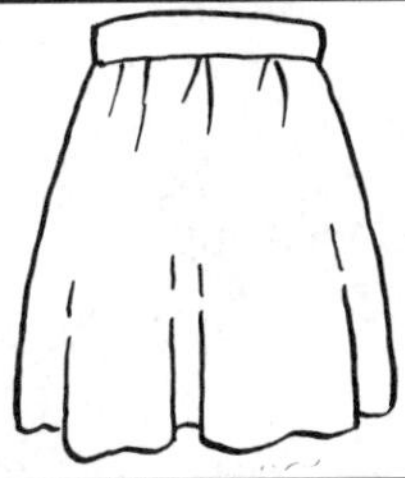
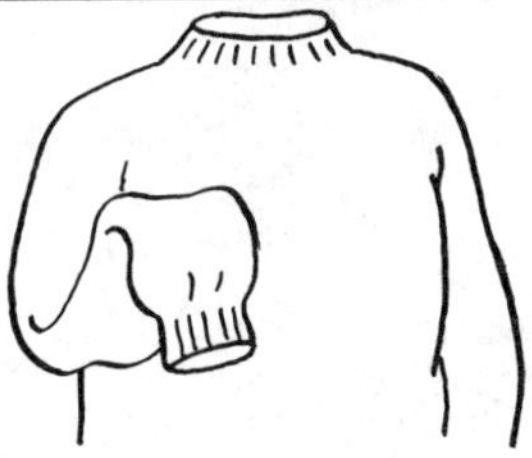
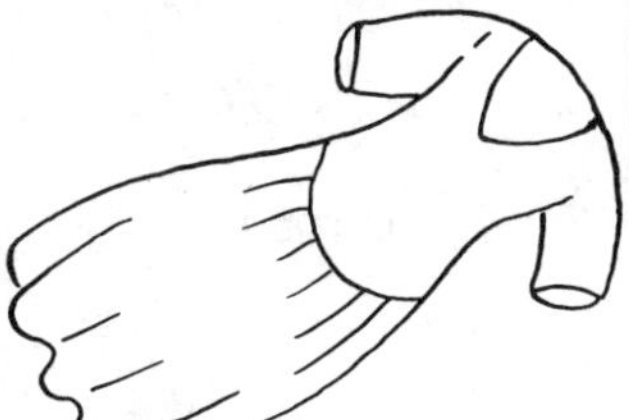
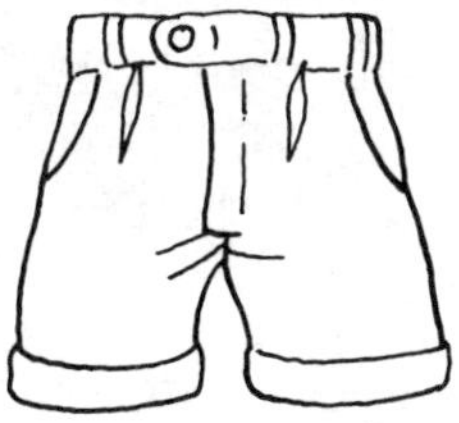
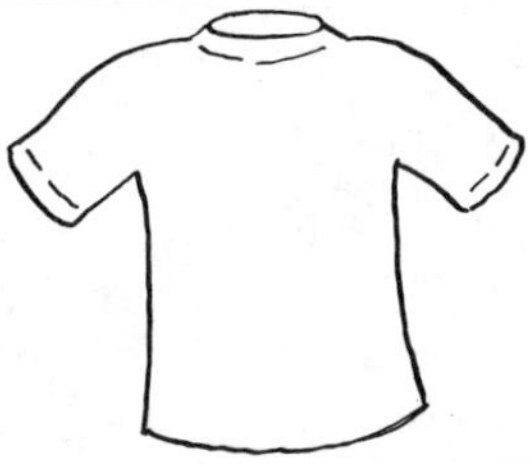
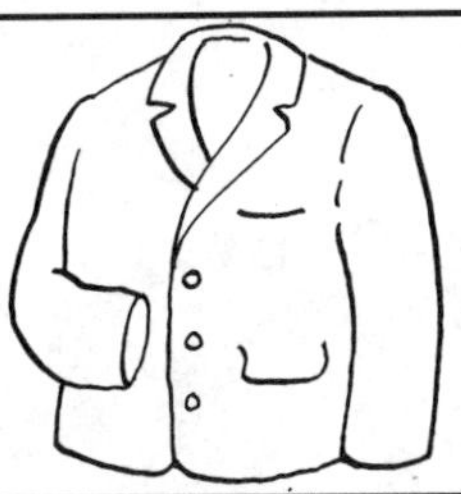

| | | travailler dans un magasin | livrer les journaux |
|---|---|---|---|
| les magazines | les disques | les cassettes | les bonbons |
| | | le match de foot | les vêtements |
| la chemise | les chaussures | les chaussettes | le chapeau |
| le jean | l'écharpe | la cravate | les collants |
| le short | la robe | le pull | la jupe |
| | | la veste | le t-shirt |
| | | | |